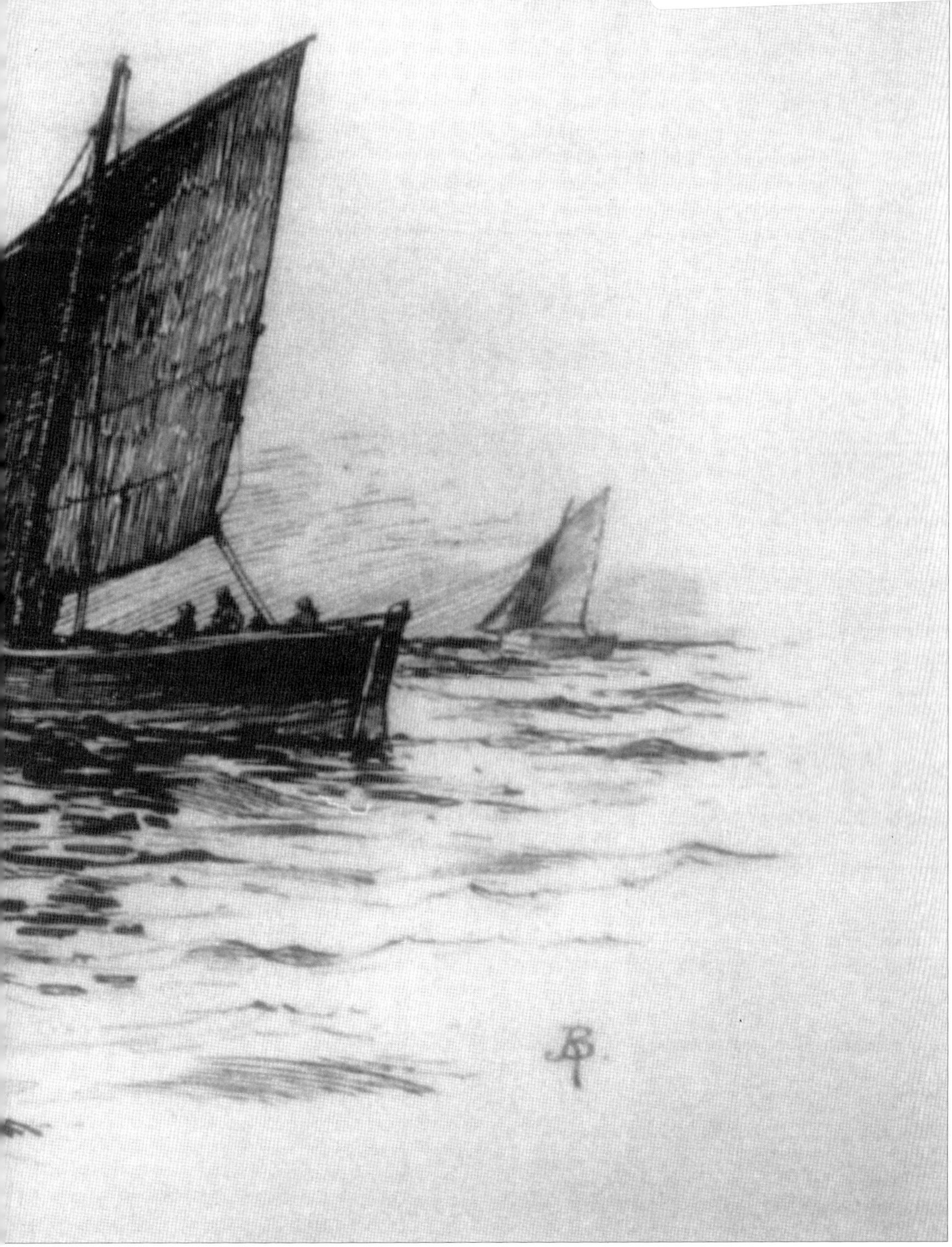

Herring boats pu
boat in the foregr

Sea Painter

The Life and Work of J.R. Bagshawe, 1870-1909

Marine Artist

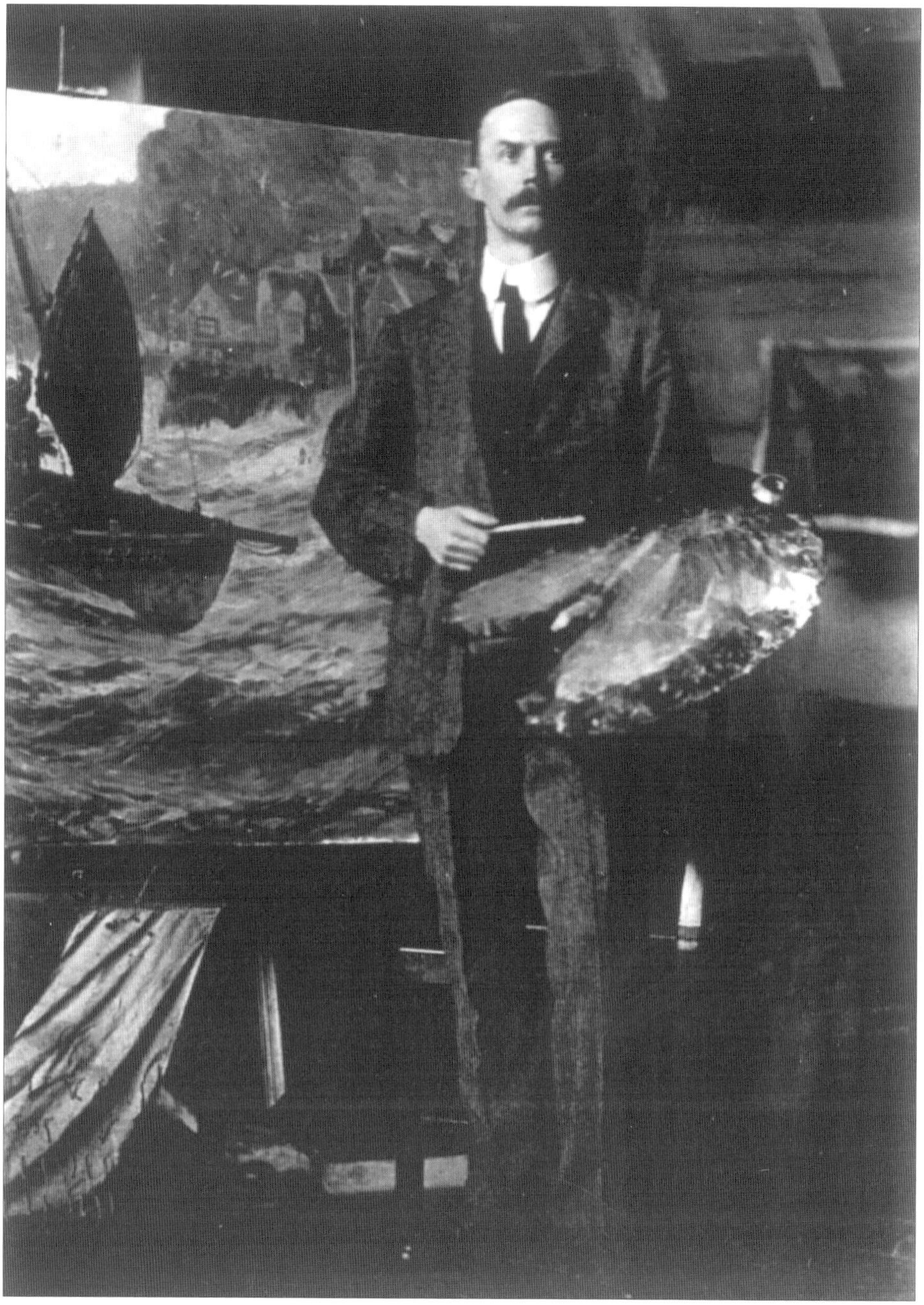

JOHN JOSEPH RICHARD BAGSHAWE
(Born Hampstead, 1 July 1870; died Whitby, 1 November 1909)

This photograph by an unknown photographer was taken in the artist's studio, which was at the rear of The Old Rectory, 23 Bagdale, Whitby. The painting on the easel was entitled Home. *It was exhibited at The Royal Academy's summer exhibition in 1905 and was considered by several critics to be one of J.R. Bagshawe's best works.*

Sea Painter

The Life and Work of J.R. Bagshawe, 1870-1909

Marine Artist

Peter Frank

Phillimore

2010

Published by
PHILLIMORE & CO. LTD
Chichester, West Sussex, England
www.phillimore.co.uk

ISBN 978-1-86077-617-5

Printed and bound in Great Britain
Manufacturing managed by
Jellyfish Print Solutions Ltd

Contents

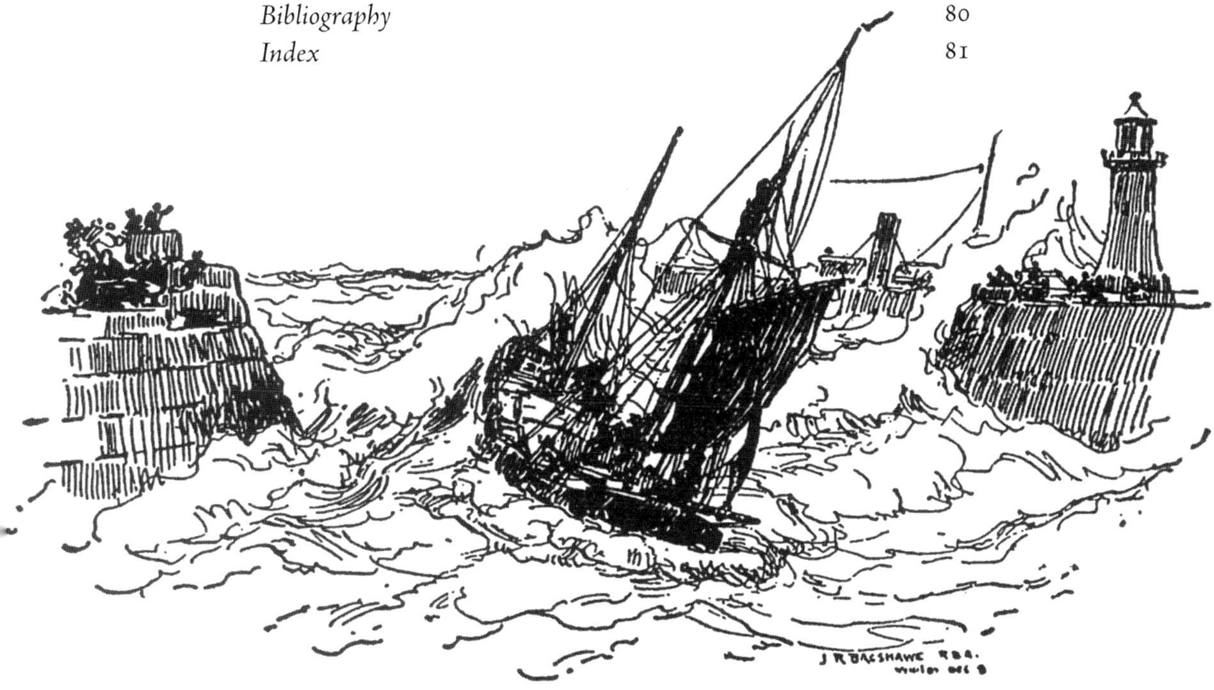

For
Victoria, Harriet and Lucy;
Owen and Colin;
Olive and Joseph.

List of Illustrations

Colour Plates, at pp.52-3

Illustration Acknowledgements

Author's collection, 49; Bagshawe family archive, endpapers, 13, 33; T.B. and R. Jordan, 46; National Army Museum, London, 11; National Portrait Gallery, London, 1; Rochdale Art Gallery, 32; J.T. Ross, 16, 18, 22, 29, 36, 37; S. Smith, Pickering, 30; Private Collection, Somerleyton Hall, Suffolk, 2; Sutcliffe Gallery, 24; Whitby Literary and Philosophical Society, 34.

Colour Plate Section:

Bagshawe family archive, 5, 15; Pannett Art Gallery, Whitby, 4; *Toilers of the Sea* series, 7, 11, 12, 13; Walker Galleries, Harrogate, 2.

Preface

As an artist, Joseph Bagshawe's preoccupation was with the sea; the sea in all its moods and in all its states: turbulence, calm, oily swell and angry storm – all are to be found in his work. His other, human, focus was those who sailed upon the sea and derived their living from it, especially the fisherfolk and their families; above all, those who dwelt on the shores of the North Sea, and, in particular, those of the North Yorkshire coast. The village of Staithes and the port of Whitby captured his attention most of all, and he earned the respect of those communities both as a person and as an artist. Yet Joseph Bagshawe was not a native of either place: in fact, he was born in Hampstead, the son of a judge and grandson of the famous marine artist Clarkson Stanfield (1793-1867), and first visited the Yorkshire coast only in his mid-twenties. He quickly established himself as a founding member and the first Secretary of the Staithes Group of Artists, a loosely organised band of painters who for a number of years were producing some of the most exciting art in Britain. Today, the work of the Staithes Group is much sought after and prices for individual paintings are rising. Bagshawe's are particularly popular, yet, in contrast to several of his fellow artists, not a great deal is known about him.

I first became aware of Joseph Bagshawe and his work in the 1980s while researching my book, *Yorkshire Fisherfolk* (Chichester: Phillimore & Co. Ltd, 2002). Over two decades I accumulated an extensive archive of mainly photographic images to serve as illustrations to the text. The problem was that, although photographs and paintings of fishermen and fisherwomen at their work on shore proved to be relatively forthcoming, images of the fishermen at sea were extremely scarce; until, that is, I came across the work of Joseph Bagshawe.

It happened like this. A principal source of photographic images was old postcards. The worldwide mania for collecting picture postcards coincided with the most productive years of the Staithes group (roughly 1902-9). Bagshawe was invited by the renowned postcard publisher Raphael Tuck & Sons to submit two sets of six watercolours each for reproduction under the general title *Toilers of the Sea*. These 12 cards (it took nearly 20 years to trace all of them) were of considerable merit artistically and also conveyed what contemporary photographs failed to do, namely, conjure the tension of men pitting themselves against the elements, thus providing a sense of what it was like to actually sail the northern sea. I decided then that, one day, I would try to find out more about Joseph Bagshawe as a person and about his work.

Bagshawe was a young artist who died at a tragically early age. Most of his contemporaries would outlast him by many years, not just in terms of their life-span, but also in their working lives. His friend Frederic Stuart Richardson (with whom he was to go on painting visits to Holland and the Channel coast) was born in 1855, 15 years before Bagshawe, but lived until 1934, thus dying 25 years after him. Laura Knight, although seven years his junior, lived until 1970, having survived her friend by 61 years.

Bagshawe was only 39 years old at the time of his death in 1909. By then, his enormous talent was being recognised: he had been elected a member of the Royal Society of British Artists; and, between 1897 and 1910, 17 of his paintings (one was hung posthumously) had been chosen for display at Royal Academy Summer Exhibitions. One can only speculate as to the extent his talents would have blossomed and flourished over another 20 or 30 years. Moreover, in the last year of his life, Joseph Bagshawe began to demonstrate a not inconsiderable literary talent in the form of journal articles that nicely complemented his artistic work and it is not inconceivable that this could have led to something more substantial. It was a tragedy that he died so young, a great loss to his wife and children, to the local community, and to British art.

Perhaps it was because he died at such an early age that Joseph Bagshawe has not always received the attention he deserves and the present volume, therefore, is a modest attempt to repair that neglect, particularly since in recent years interest in the Staithes Group of Artists has grown steadily and with it curiosity about Bagshawe. Of inestimable help in researching this topic has been the enthusiastic cooperation of Nicholas and Daphne Bagshawe (Nicholas is a grandson of Joseph Bagshawe): in the most hospitable fashion they welcomed me into their home, laid out an abundance of memorabilia, notebooks and sketchbooks, not to mention allowing me to photograph many of the Bagshawe paintings in their possession, paintings that are well-represented in the present volume (indicated in the captions, where appropriate, as being from the 'Bagshawe family archive').

Also, at the very beginning of my enquiries into the life and art of Joseph Bagshawe, Christine Pybus, a Whitby-based artist of repute and an enthusiastic admirer of the Staithes Group, kindly directed me towards several documentary sources that proved to be an excellent launch pad for subsequent research. I am grateful, too, to Ian Walker of the Walker Galleries, Harrogate, who responded instantly to my plea for help, most notably by supplying me with an extensive catalogue of a sale of Bagshawe paintings, as well as a personal recollection of the Bagshawe family.

Since I am incompetent with most things technical, including photographic equipment, I was desperately in need of assistance in assembling images of persons and places associated with Joseph Bagshawe. In that respect, to my rescue came James Willis, who, an artist himself, is a wizard at photographic imaging: he photographed and meticulously copied and processed many of the illustrations for this book. To him, too, I am extremely grateful.

James Dodds of Wivenhoe, Essex, is one of Britain's most distinguished and exciting contemporary marine artists, with whom I was privileged to have several fascinating conversations about Bagshawe. The insights he provided and his acute perceptions of Bagshawe's work – its social significance as well as artistic – triggered several productive lines of thought (although, needless to say, any shortcomings in the assessment and analysis of Bagshawe's work are entirely my responsibility).

Despite the valuable help I received from all these people, there remain several unanswered questions and not a few 'black holes' in the narrative. For example, Joseph Bagshawe's love of Ireland and the Irish is all too obvious, yet it has proved to be impossible to find out precisely how and why he came to be so passionately drawn to Connemara. Still, this account would be all the more deficient had I not had the ready help of those mentioned above. Finally, I doubt that the book would have seen the light of day were it not that my wife, Mary, and our children have encouraged, cajoled and chivvied me into bringing it to completion; to them, as always, I am extremely grateful.

Peter Frank
Colchester, 2010

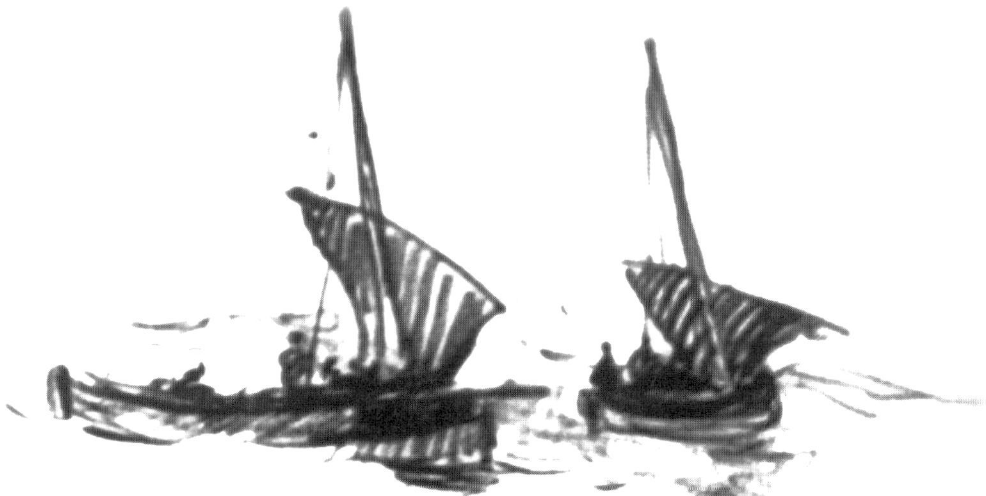

One
The Making of an Artist: First Steps

'In writing of an artist the first points to be considered are the influences which have moved him. In the case of Joseph Bagshawe, his principal motive may be said to have been "in the blood". A grandson of Clarkson Stanfield, R.A., the friend of Turner, the painter of innumerable pictures of shipping and the sea, we may say our artist was "born with a brush in his hand, and the sea for a subject"'. So wrote fellow artist Hirst Walker shortly after his friend's untimely death in 1909.[1]

That Joseph Bagshawe's life and art were influenced by the fame and reputation of his maternal grandfather there can be little doubt. Such was the eminence of Clarkson Stanfield that, even though he died three years before Joseph was born, he must surely have been a major artistic and cultural presence within the Bagshawe family circle and thus eventually a powerful factor in Joseph's decision to become a painter.

Stanfield's life was the stuff of which family legends are made.[2] His father (Joseph Bagshawe's great grandfather), James Stanfield, was Irish. Born in Dublin, he later studied for the priesthood in France, but, giving that up, moved to Liverpool and signed on as a seaman. June 1775 found him in Benin, where he enlisted as a crew member of a ship carrying slaves from West Africa to Jamaica, returning to Liverpool the following year.[3] Appalled by what he had witnessed, he came ashore and joined the abolitionists. Subsequently, he became an actor, playwright and author. James Stanfield's wife (*née* Hoad) was an actress and also an artist: she taught painting and it was she, it is said, who started their son Clarkson on his career as an artist.

Clarkson was born in Sunderland in 1793, but in 1806, at the age of 13, he was apprenticed to a heraldic painter in Edinburgh. He stayed in that job for two years, before giving it up and going to sea in the merchant service. Despite Nelson's famous victory over the French and Spanish fleets off Cape Trafalgar, hostilities continued intermittently between England and France and it was against that background that Clarkson in 1812 was pressed into the Royal Navy. He served for two years before being discharged as unfit, having injured himself by falling from the rigging of his ship. However, his injury cannot have been too serious since, soon after, he sailed in a merchant vessel for China, returning to England a year later.

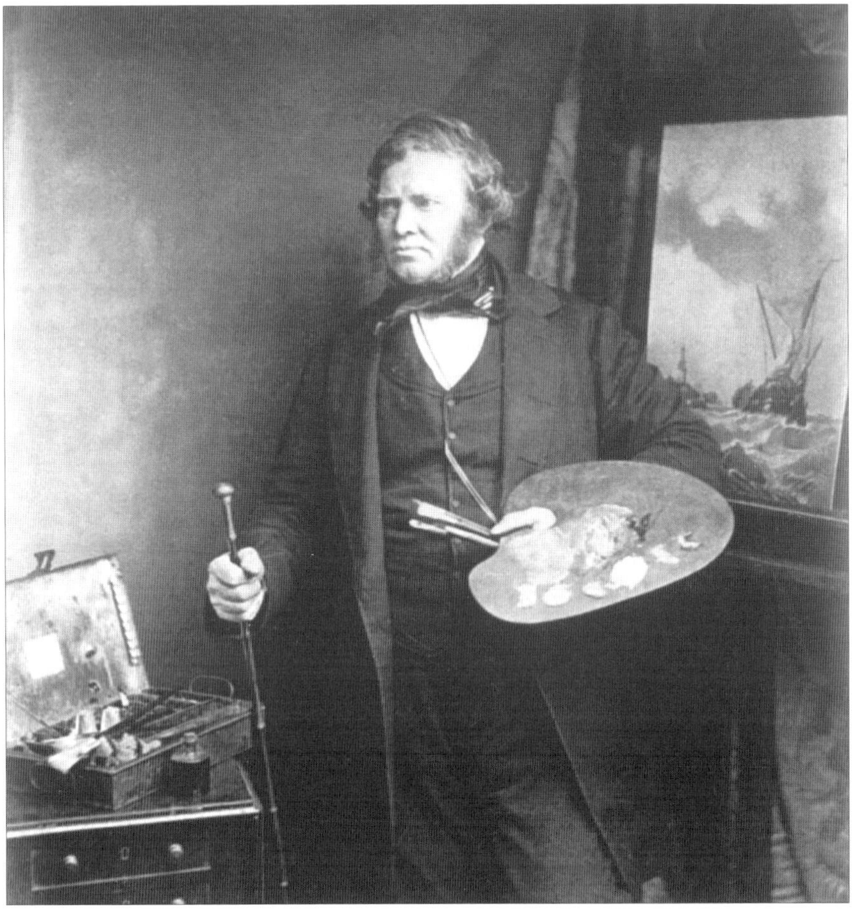

1 Clarkson Stanfield, R.A.

Clarkson Stanfield (1793-1867) was J.R. Bagshawe's maternal grandfather. This photograph of him was taken by the Victorian photographer William Lake Price. It depicts the artist standing in front of a painting entitled A Dutch Blazer Coming Out of Monnickendam. *A much larger version hangs in the Garrick Club in London, of which, in 1831, Stanfield was a founder member; it is inscribed 'Painted For and Presented to the Garrick Club/Decr. 1856 by Clarkson Stanflield, R.A.'. It was not unusual for artists to do more than one version of a painting, either to retain, or to sell. This one is a splendid rendition of sea and sky, for which Stanfield was famed.*

Life on board ship could be dreary and monotonous. Distractions were few and boredom could give rise to mischief, so captains were glad on long voyages to improvise entertainments for their crews. Nelson, for example, in the prolonged periods of inactivity while waiting for the French and Spanish fleets to leave port and do battle on the open sea, instructed his captains to stage theatricals on board their ships.[4]

It was while serving in the Royal Navy and then during the voyages to and from China on the merchantman that Clarkson Stanfield began to develop his talent as an artist by painting scenery for shipboard productions. At the same time, he started to produce small marine subjects that attracted the attention of his superior officers. Thus encouraged, he came ashore in 1816 to begin a new career as a scene painter at The Royalty Theatre in east London.

Two years later, Clarkson married a woman called Mary Hutchinson and they had two children. Mary died young and in 1824 or 1825 he married Rebecca Adcock: they were to have 10 children: eight boys and two girls. The seventh child, and the eldest daughter, Harriet, was destined to be Joseph Bagshawe's mother.

Meanwhile, Clarkson's career as a theatrical scene painter flourished and it was not long before he moved to Drury Lane in the West End. He continued to do marine paintings in oils and enjoyed such success that eventually he gave up scene painting altogether (except that later he did scenery for amateur productions put on by his close friends, the novelists Charles Dickens and Wilkie Collins) and concentrated on easel painting. He was a founder member of the Society of British Artists, becoming its President in 1829, and three years later was elected an Associate Member of the Royal Academy (A.R.A.) and, three years after that, in 1835, a full Royal Academician (R.A.).

Clarkson Stanfield was patronised first by William IV and then by Queen Victoria. It was William, for example, who invited him to record the opening by the King of the new London Bridge and of Portsmouth Harbour. But it was his paintings of Trafalgar that brought Stanfield popular acclaim. His massive depiction in 1836 of *The Battle of Trafalgar*, reminiscent in its scale and technique of his earlier scenery painting, was immensely popular (it was purchased by the United Services Club in Pall Mall – now the Institute of Directors, where it hangs to this day), and it was followed some 20 years later by *H.M.S.* Victory, *with the body of Nelson on board, towed into Gibraltar, 28th October 1805, seven days after the Battle of Trafalgar* (private collection, Somerleyton Hall, Suffolk). In *Trafalgar*, the movement, the turbulence, is in the clash between the British and French and Spanish fleets; whereas in *Victory* it lies in the rendering of the sea and the sky, as well as in the poignancy of the subject. Then in 1863 there came his *The Morning after Trafalgar* (purchased in 1889 by the National Gallery of Victoria, Australia). And there were numerous other works on maritime themes, less heroic, it is true, but all displaying a consummate understanding of the ever-changing moods of sea and sky. Indeed, Stanfield was considered to be second only to Turner in his treatment of cloud forms, while John Ruskin judged him to be 'the leader of the English realists' and drew particular attention to his truthfully observed skies and his astonishing ability to render the movement and transparency of water.

But if the sea and ships were Stanfield's first love, he did not neglect other subjects. There were the paintings he made on his travels at home and abroad, and his illustrations for novels by Captain Marryat and by his friend Charles Dickens, who dedicated *Little Dorrit* to him. Indeed, upon Stanfield's death in May 1867, it was the great writer who penned the valedictory eulogy that was published in his journal *All the Year Round*. England, wrote Dickens, has lost:

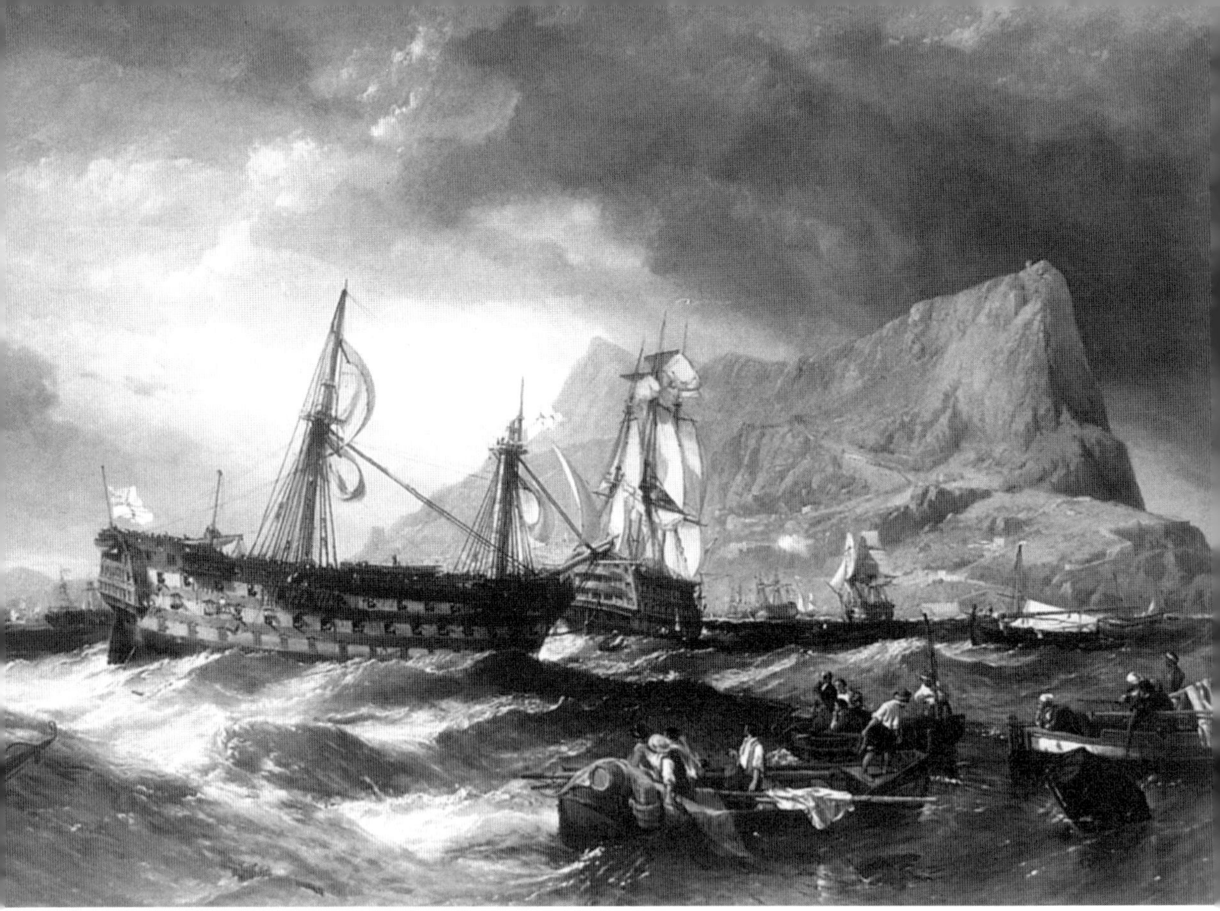

2 H.M.S. *Victory* by Clarkson Stanfield (1793-1867)

The full title of this painting is H.M.S. Victory, with the body of Nelson on board, towed into Gibraltar, 28th October 1805, seven days after the Battle of Trafalgar. *It was exhibited at the Royal Academy in 1853.*

Stanfield (Joseph Bagshawe's maternal grandfather and an inspiration to him) was noted, as the critic John Ruskin put it, for his 'truthfully observed skies and his astonishing ability to render the movement and transparency of water'. Charles Dickens described him after his death as 'the National Historian of the sea', the 'greatest marine painter of whom she [England] will be boastful ages hence'. Although Stanfield was long since, justly, outshone by his friend J.M.W. Turner, he remains one of Britain's most distinguished marine artists.

> The greatest marine painter of whom she will be boastful ages hence; the National Historian of her speciality, the Sea; the man famous in all countries for the marvellous rendering of the waves that break upon her shores, of her ships and seamen, of her coasts and skies, of her storms and sunshine, of the many marvels of the deep.[5]

So, how could Joseph Bagshawe not be proudly conscious of his grandfather's fame, of the affection and esteem in which he was held by so many of the great writers, artists and critics of the age, not to mention an admiring public that extended throughout the land and included the monarch herself? All families, given the opportunity, venerate their heroes, and the Bagshawes were no exception. That, too, was to have a decisive influence on Joseph's character and artistic development. But there was yet another important factor associated with his grandfather that was to play a vital role in many aspects of Joseph's life – although very rarely in his art – and that was religion.

Clarkson Stanfield converted to Catholicism and was re-baptised on 3 October 1846; his wife converted at the same time.[6] He appears to have been devout, yet no zealot, although it is said that his friends, while still enjoying his company, learned to avoid discussion relating to religion. However, he and his wife's adoption of the Catholic faith did mean that his children were also baptised Catholics, which in turn to some extent determined whom they would marry.

William Henry Gunning Bagshawe also came from a Catholic background. His father, Henry Ridgard Bagshawe (1799-1870), was a distinguished lawyer who incurred the displeasure of his relatives by converting to the Roman Catholic faith. Educated at Oakham and Richmond grammar schools, he went up to Trinity College, Cambridge, taking his degree in 1822 and entering the Middle Temple three years later. In the meantime, in 1824, at the Chapel of the British Ambassador in Paris, he had married Catherine Elizabeth Gunning, daughter of John Gunning, Wellington's Inspector General of Hospitals and Surgeon Extraordinary to King George IV.

It was not until 1838 that Henry Ridgard was confirmed into the Catholic Church, but soon after he became a prolific writer of articles for the *Dublin Review*. Appointed a Queen's Counsel, he later became a judge of the county courts of Cardigan, Carmarthen and Pembroke and subsequently of the Clerkenwell District of London. He had the distinction of being the first Roman Catholic judge to be appointed since the Reformation.

There are several versions of the story as to how Henry Ridgard converted to Catholicism. One has it that, as a child, he was indoctrinated by an Irish maid. Another claims that a Mr Dolman, an editor of the *Dublin Review*, following one of his frequent visits to the Bagshawe house, left behind samples of Catholic literature which duly influenced Henry. And the third version is that four of Henry's children were sent off to Derbyshire to stay with relations and while there a daughter was observed making the sign of the cross, whereupon the relations urged Henry to hunt out and expel a presumed Papist servant. It turned out, however, that it was Henry's own wife, who had been confirmed in 1832, who had covertly introduced Roman Catholicism into the family.

Once this became known to the Derbyshire relations, they urged Henry, in the biblical phrase, to 'put his wife away' (at that time divorce was practically unheard of). Henry asked to be allowed a year in which to study the Bible and reflect upon this suggestion, but, after that year was up, he, too, converted and was subsequently to play a prominent role in the restoration of the Catholic Hierarchy, which took place in 1850. Apparently, it was from Henry Ridgard's house in London's Fitzroy Square that Dr Wiseman set out for Rome, and to which he returned, as Cardinal, the first Archbishop of Westminster.

Henry Ridgard's son, William Henry Gunning Bagshawe, married Clarkson Stanfield's daughter, Harriet Theresa, in 1861 and they set up home at 46 Belsize Square in Hampstead. They were an up-and-coming, prosperous, professional middle-class family. William, son of a distinguished lawyer and himself a barrister at law with chambers at 5 New Square, Lincoln's Inn, and Harriet, daughter of a renowned Royal Academician, made a good match. They lived in a substantial house in this increasingly fashionable west London suburb: it had three storeys, plus a basement and attics, and was entered through an imposing portico (today, following years of decline, the street is showing signs of re-gentrification). It was here on 1 July 1870 that Joseph John Richard Bagshawe was born, William and Harriet's second son and fourth child (there were to be 11 altogether: big families were not unusual in those days, but the fact that the Bagshawes were Catholics and therefore unlikely to favour birth control may have had something to do with their having so many children – what was perhaps more unusual was that all survived to maturity).

Nothing is known about Joseph's early childhood. He was born in the same year that W.E. Foster's Education Act was passed, but it is extremely unlikely that the Bagshawes would send their children to an ordinary Board school, so the probability is that Joseph was either tutored at home or attended a local private school. By the time the 1881 national census came along the Bagshawe family had moved the quite short distance to 182 Haverstock Hill, a house not unlike 45 Belsize Square, except that it was more spacious, doubtless to accommodate an ever-growing family, and much closer to the main part of Hampstead (it, too, is now multi-occupied and run-down, although many similar properties in the neighbourhood seem to be being refurbished and reverting to one-family ownership). Today, number 182 is immediately adjacent to Belsize Park tube station (opened in 1907), but when the Bagshawes lived there Haverstock Hill still enjoyed an air of quiet gentility, as is captured in Sir George Clausen's popular *Spring Morning: Haverstock Hill* (1881, Bury Art Gallery).

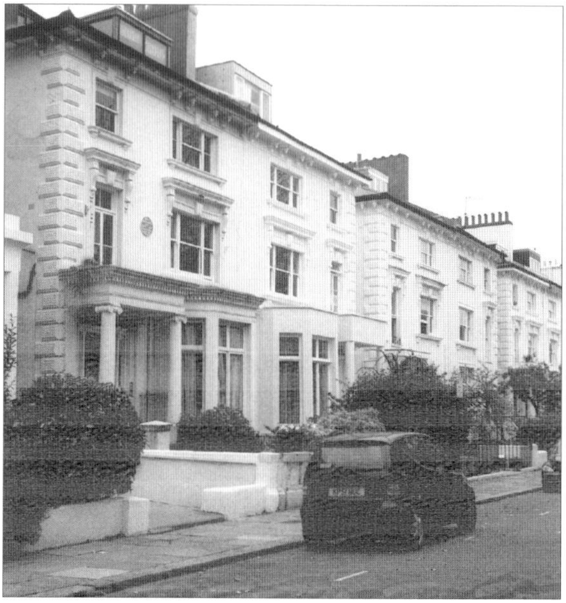

3 46 Belsize Square, Hampstead

The house at 46 Belsize Square, Hampstead (to the left of the parked car in the foreground), where, on 1 July 1870, Joseph Bagshawe was born. His father, William Henry Gunning Bagshawe, was a barrister. Later, the family moved a short distance to a similar, but somewhat larger property at 182 Haverstock Hill.

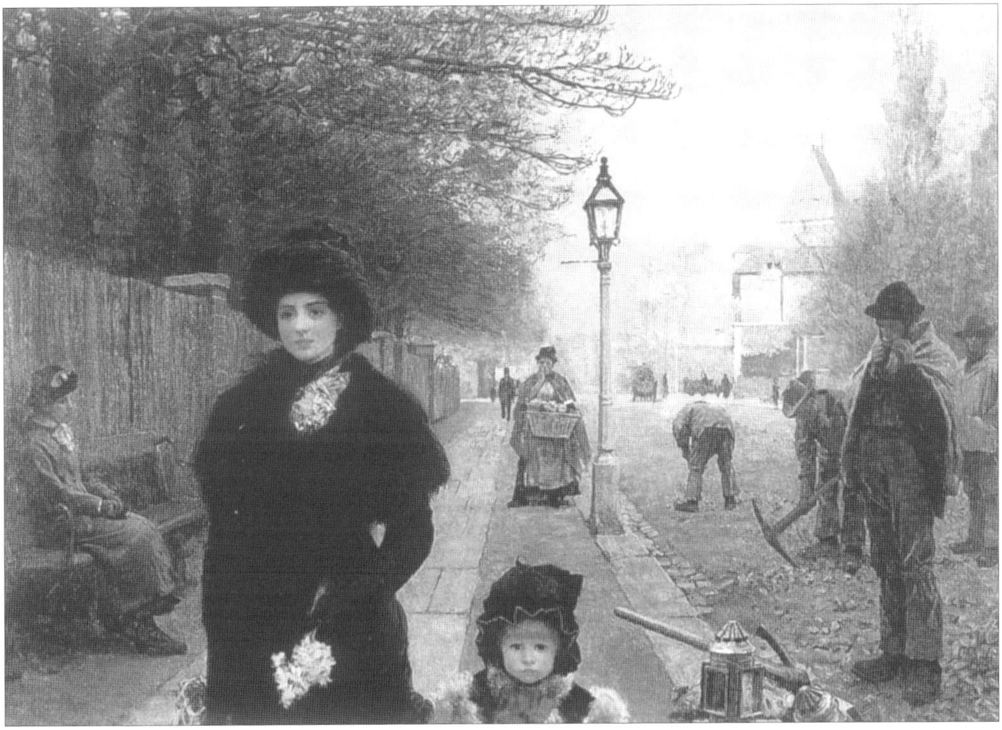

4 HAVERSTOCK HILL, HAMPSTEAD, IN THE 1880S

Hampstead in the 1870s and 1880s was a well-to-do, rising neighbourhood much favoured by writers, artists and the professional classes. A resident at that time was Sir George Clausen (1852-1944), whose Spring Morning: Haverstock Hill, 1881 *(Bury Art Gallery), conveys nicely both the gentility and rapid development of the area. This was the milieu in which Joseph Bagshawe spent his early boyhood.*

Joseph left home at the age of 12 on 21 September 1882 to enrol at St Augustine's College, Ramsgate, Kent. He was to remain there until May 1885.

The choice of St Augustine's was almost certainly influenced, albeit posthumously, by his maternal grandfather. Amongst Clarkson Stanfield's wide circle of friends in the arts was Augustus Welby Northmore Pugin (1812-52). Pugin was one of the leading architects of the 19th century. He designed furniture for Windsor Castle when just 15 years old, then, briefly, he created sets for the London theatre (something that he and Clarkson Stanfield had in common), before marrying and moving to Salisbury. It was there that in 1835 he converted to Catholicism (a second parallel with Stanfield) and wrote a celebrated book, *Contrasts*. This was followed six years later by the publication of *The True Principles of Christian or Pointed Architecture*. By 'pointed architecture' was meant the Gothic style and Pugin became one of the principal exponents of the so-called Gothic Revival. He went on to produce numerous designs for churches and cathedrals, as well as some for domestic buildings. It was he who inspired the design of the Medieval Court at the Great Exhibition of 1851, which was visited specially by Queen Victoria and Prince Albert; but, above all, he is remembered for having earlier conceived the elaborate interiors of the Houses of Parliament when they were rebuilt following the disastrous fire of 1834.

It was Pugin's passion for medieval architecture, together with his zeal as a Christian, that inspired his art. As has been pointed out,[7] he believed that morality and art had been indivisible in the Middle Ages and that good art and architecture were produced by men whose souls were pure. Following on from this theory, Pugin damned the Renaissance as a period of 'pagan art' produced by a society that had turned its back on true Christian values. And so it was partly to put his theories into practice, and perhaps even more as an act of personal devotion, that in 1843 he embarked upon the building of his 'own' church at Ramsgate.

It was Pugin's church in the sense that he designed it, paid for it, and built it. He named it after St Augustine (in other words, it was his own name-saint's church) who had brought Christianity to southern England and whose archbishopric was at nearby Canterbury. It is considered by many modern architectural historians to be one of the most important churches in Britain.[8]

The history of St Augustine's Abbey Church – to give it its full title – is comprehensively covered in Horner and Hunter's *A Flint Seaside Church* (2000) published by the Pugin Society, and in Rosemary Hill's biography of Pugin, *God's Architect* (2007).[9] Suffice to say briefly for present purposes that this remarkable church is built of grey, knapped flint with stone dressings. The flint is local, but the sandstone came by sea from quarries near Whitby in Yorkshire. Adjacent to St Augustine's, and also looking out onto the Channel and Pegwell Bay, is the house Pugin had built for himself, The Grange; while to the rear and across the road that runs behind the church stands St Augustine's Abbey, built in 1860-1, after Pugin's death, by his son E.W. Pugin.

Immediately upon completion, St Augustine's Abbey became home for a community of Benedictine monks who, partly in order to finance the running and upkeep of the Abbey, opened a school for boys. It was here that Joseph Bagshawe arrived in September 1882.

Clarkson Stanfield and Pugin were close friends (although the precise circumstances of their becoming acquainted are not known) and Stanfield was a frequent visitor to The Grange. While Pugin was, of course, primarily an author and architect, he was not without talent as an artist, albeit mainly of architectural illustration. He was also passionately interested in the sea and those who sailed upon it. The Grange has a tower from which Pugin would look out towards the treacherous Goodwin Sands, watching for boats in trouble in stormy weather; and he was especially concerned for the welfare – material and spiritual – of shipwrecked mariners who were brought ashore at Ramsgate.

Pugin's interest in boats was long-standing. Well before moving to the coast, in the 1820s, he had kept his own boat, the *Elizabeth*, on the Thames; later, in 1849, he became part-owner of a lugger, the *Caroline*, that sailed out of Ramsgate. This was a quite substantial vessel, three-masted, 40 feet long, 13 feet wide and clench built (that is, with her planks overlapping, rather than meeting edge to edge).

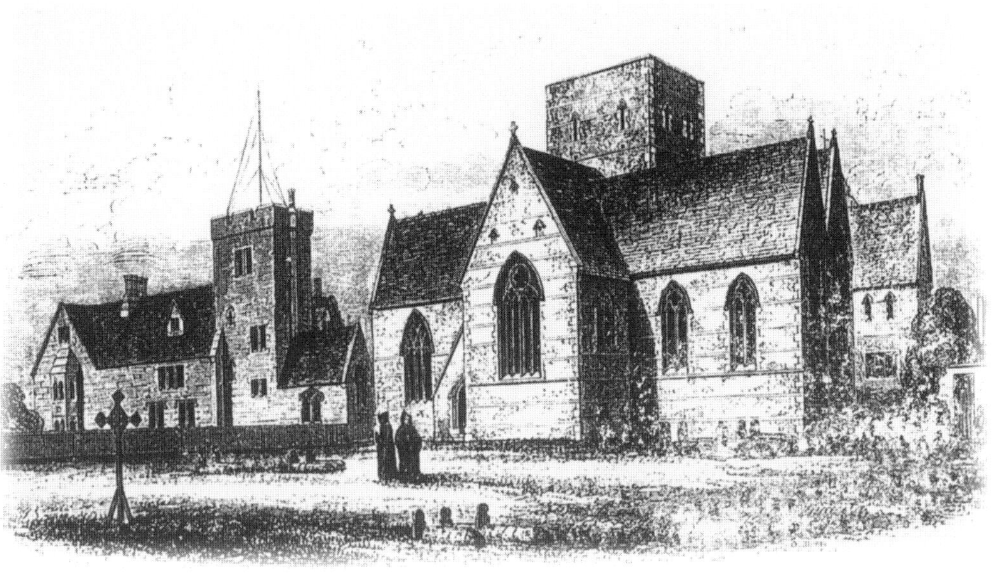

5 Saint Augustine's Abbey Church, Ramsgate

Augustus Welby Northmore Pugin (1812-42) was the principal exponent of Gothic revivalist architecture. As a youth he designed furniture for Windsor Castle and later the interiors of the new Houses of Parliament. Towards the end of his tragically short life, Pugin designed and had built St Augustine's Abbey Church on the West Cliff at Ramsgate, together with, alongside, his private dwelling, The Grange.

The illustration above is taken from Benjamin Ferrey's Recollections of A.N. Welby Pugin, *1861, as reproduced in Libby Horner and Gill Hunter's* A Flint Seaside Church *(Ramsgate: The Pugin Society, 2000). The Grange is on the left.*

Soon after Pugin's death, his son Edward built a Benedictine monastery, also named after St Augustine, just across the road at the rear of the Abbey Church, which soon became a school for boys run by the monks. Augustus Pugin and Clarkson Stanfield (both Catholic converts) were friends; which probably explains why Joseph Bagshawe's parents chose to send their son to St Augustine's, where he was a pupil from September 1882 to May 1885.

It seems that the *Caroline* was as much – perhaps more – an investment than purely for pleasure, since it was used both for ferrying supplies to ships anchoring in the relatively sheltered stretch of water that lies between the cliffs of Kent and the Goodwins, and for salvaging goods from vessels that had run aground on the Sands. Doubtless this shared passion for the sea was yet another factor that drew Stanfield and Pugin together.

Pugin died young in 1852, Stanfield in 1867, yet it is quite likely that Joseph Bagshawe's mother, Harriet, born in 1838, had heard her father speak about Pugin and Ramsgate (she may even have visited The Grange with him), so that when the time came for her and her husband as good Catholic parents to decide where to send their son to boarding school, where better than to St Augustine's?

No record survives of Joseph's academic performance at St Augustine's, apart from a few pages in a ledger showing when he was enrolled at the school and when he left, together with accounts listing any expenses incurred over and above the fees.[10] The charge for 'Pension in advance for One Quarter' in Joseph's first term came to £13 2s. 6d. (an amount that remained constant throughout his stay at St Augustine's), but in addition there was, for example, a guinea for laundry, 2s. 6d. for stationery, 1s. 6d. for an excursion to Margate, and another 1s. 6d. for three haircuts. There were also various textbooks to be purchased, including an English grammar, a French grammar, as well as a Bible History and an Introduction to Geography. Altogether that first quarter the bill presented to Joseph's father amounted to £14 16s. 6d.

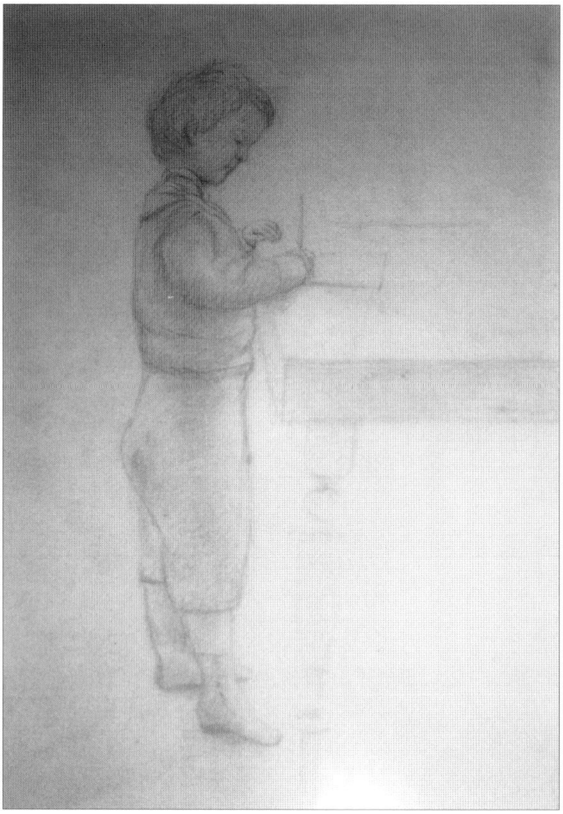

6 First Signs

Joseph's interest in art seems to have manifested itself at an early age. In the Bagshawe family archive there is a pencil sketch by Joseph's father showing Joseph as a small boy (perhaps seven or eight years old) standing at a table drawing. While at St Augustine's he seems to have further developed his interest in painting and may, even then, have begun to consider art as a possible career.

The charges for subsequent quarters followed roughly the same pattern, except that, with extras, the sums quickly rose to a fairly consistent £26. For a start, clothing and footwear begin to feature quite prominently, as does extra food (Joseph appears to have had a fondness for chops, not to mention 'Ale for dinner', eggs and biscuits, from which it may be deduced that he and his appetite were growing quickly as he entered adolescence). Also, in the fourth quarter of 1884 two new items appear: a cricket 'jacket' and cricket trousers, an early indication of his fondness for a sport that was never to desert him.

The accounts presented to Joseph's father itemised expenditures on what nowadays might be termed 'non-core subjects' – those extra to the then main curriculum – such as foreign languages, music and chemistry. Listed, too, is 'Drawing', against which there is no entry until the last quarter of 1883, when materials appropriate to that subject are charged: paper, pencil case, portfolio, rubber and such. But in the quarter ending 21 June 1884 to the printed entry 'Drawing' is added in manuscript '*& painting*', followed by, amongst other sundries, 'Box of water colours' at 19s. 6d., a very considerable sum at that time. The next term, there is an unspecified charge against Drawing of 42s. (one wonders whether it was for special tuition), together with another item 'Drawing mounts 1s. 6d.'. There is also in the Bagshawe family archive a pencil sketch by Joseph's father of his son as a boy of perhaps just eight or nine years, standing at a desk with a pencil in his hand, drawing; so it could be that these school expenditures are indications of a continuing and developing interest in and talent for art.

If it *is* correct to assume that it was while at St Augustine's that Joseph became seriously interested in painting, then what might have been the environmental factors that influenced him? There is no evidence whatsoever to suggest that the religious atmosphere engendered by the monks who taught him, and the fact that the College was a religious, as well as an educational, establishment had any profound effect upon him artistically (although for the whole of his life he remained a devout Catholic). However, it is possible that the broader, physical environment was more influential in the development of his art.

St Augustine's Church, The Grange and the Abbey stand atop the chalk cliffs on the west side of Ramsgate with the land at their backs and their faces to the sea. Between them and the cliff edge stretches a promenade that was a favourite walk for the more well-to-do visitor. Not far offshore lie the Goodwin Sands, parts of which dry out at certain low tides – Joseph may have been familiar with his grandfather's painting of the Sands (it was reproduced in *The Illustrated London News* in 1859). Between the Goodwins and the shore runs a channel of deeper water, the Downs, which affords a haven for shipping in stormy weather. It was here, too, that vessels lay to take on pilots to navigate them into the estuary and up the Thames. Similarly, fleets would sometimes rendezvous in the Downs before setting sail to do battle in times of war. Even today it is not unusual for that popular sailors' song 'Spanish Ladies' to be sung at commemorative Trafalgar Day dinners, with its rousing verses:

We'll rant and we'll roar like true British sailors.
We'll range and we'll roam across the salt seas,
Until we strike soundings in the Channel of old England,
From Ushant to Scilly is thirty-five leagues.

Then on up the Channel until:

... The signal was made for the grand fleet to anchor,
All in the Downs that night for to meet;
Then it's stand by your stoppers, let go your shank painters,
Haul all your clew garnets, stick out tacks and sheets.

Such sentiments are far from everyone's taste in post-imperial Britain, but to a young boy whose grandfather had been the artist-chronicler of some of the country's greatest moments in her maritime history, they must have been inspiring indeed (as is suggested later when Joseph began to exhibit professionally and the themes of some of his early paintings echoed those of his grandfather – although he seems to have chosen the defeat of the Spanish armada, rather than Trafalgar, as his main source of inspiration). Still, what probably captured Joseph's attention as much as, if not more than, heroic images of armadas and battles was the prosaic activity of the port of Ramsgate and the traffic that passed up and down the coast.

Ramsgate in the 1880s was both a haven of refuge and a major fishing station in its own right (as well as being an established holiday resort). Its harbour was crowded with fishing smacks, part of the extensive fleet that trawled the English Channel before returning to port to sell its catch. It may well have been here that Joseph first acquired his interest in boats, in their lines, their rigging, the set of their sails and how they behaved on the sea. It was an arduous, dangerous calling, especially for the apprentices that all boats carried as part of the crew.

Many of these 'smack boys' were recruited from orphanages and reformatories. When the weather was bad and the fleet was kept in harbour these boys were forced ashore. Few had homes in which to shelter; instead they often had to seek refuge in doorways, cold, hungry and desolate. It was in an effort to ameliorate these dreadful conditions that the Sailors' Church, known originally as the Sailors' Home and Harbour Mission, was opened in 1878. It is true, the church was not concerned solely with the seafarers' and smack boys' material welfare; it was as much preoccupied with their souls. But at a time when state provision for the indigent was almost entirely lacking, the church's efforts were very welcome. Initially, smack boys when ashore were looked after in rooms above the Sailors' Church, but in 1881, the year before Joseph arrived in Ramsgate, a purpose-built Home for Smack Boys was opened alongside the church (the building still stands, although it is now devoted to other purposes).

It is hardly likely that Joseph and his fellow pupils were permitted to fraternise with smack boys – class distinction in Victorian England was too strict for that

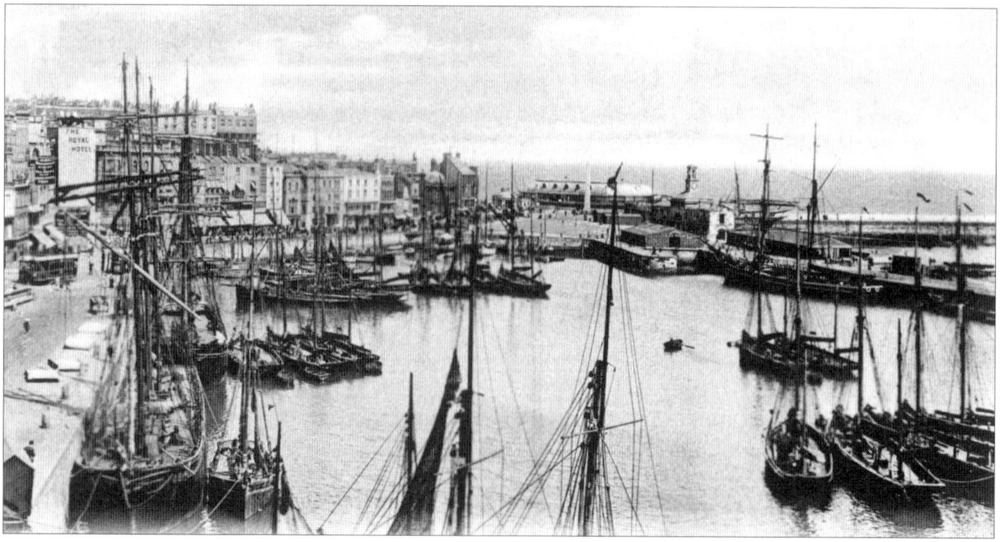

7 Ramsgate Harbour

As well as being a popular holiday resort, Ramsgate at the end of the 19th century was also a busy fishing port. Smacks such as those shown in this photograph (Valentines Series) trawled the English Channel and the southern North Sea. This must have been a familiar sight for Joseph Bagshawe when he was a pupil at St Augustine's and it was perhaps here that he first developed his interest in fishing craft and their crews, as well as the bigger vessels that passed offshore.

– but it would be remarkable if he did not compare his own position as the son of a well-to-do member of the upper middle class with the plight of these wretched boys (a supposition that is perhaps given some substance by his empathy with and sympathy for the Yorkshire fisherfolk amongst whom he later settled and whose lives and labour he painted from the mid-1890s onwards).

Joseph left St Augustine's in May 1885 to enter Beaumont College, Old Windsor, the following September. Both were Catholic educational institutions, but otherwise in terms of size and appearance they were very different. Instead of the exposed, cliff-top position overlooking the English Channel, Beaumont stood on the crest of a picturesque, wooded hill that rose gently from the banks of the River Thames. The grounds extended over nearly 200 hundred acres, parts of which were occupied by stately beech trees, except in one spot where they had been felled to provide a vista of Windsor Castle (Queen Victoria twice visited Beaumont). Eton College was only a short distance away (Beaumont was often referred to as 'the Catholic Eton'), as was Holloway College, 'an institution for the higher education of ladies', while Runnymede, with its associations with the Great Charter, was also close by.

No record has survived of Joseph's stay at Beaumont: when the college closed in the 1960s some of the pupils transferred to Stonyhurst College in Lancashire, but unfortunately no archives survived the move. However, a description of the architectural layout of Beaumont and of its academic regime at around the time Joseph was a pupil there may serve to suggest the kind of physical and intellectual environment in which he lived between 1885 and 1889.[11]

The original house at the heart of the estate had been built by Henry Frederick Thynne, who died in 1705, following which there were many changes of ownership, until eventually it became the residence of Warren Hastings, the first Governor General of India who lived there for most of the seven years he was on trial before the House of Lords, charged with corruption. Hastings sold it to a Mr Henry Griffiths who demolished most of the original house and erected the mansion that later was to become Beaumont College.

The new building was designed by an architect named Emlyn, who, inspired perhaps by nearby Windsor Castle, created a new order of 'British' architecture, so called because it was embellished by the insignia of the Order of the Garter. This is how it was described in 1894:

> The corridor contains columns 36ft.8in. high, in imitation of twin trees; in the cleft between the stems, instead of the bark, the shield of a knight is introduced, which, together with the base, is of Portland stone. The capitols are formed like the plumage of the cap worn by Knights of the Garter, with Ionic volutes interwoven together in the front, with the star of the Order between them.

The Beaumont estate was acquired by a Lord Ashbrook in 1805, in whose ownership it remained until 1854, when it was bought by the Society of Jesus, the Jesuits, initially as a home for their novitiate. Not until 1861 (coincidentally the same year that St Augustine's College in Ramsgate was established) was Beaumont turned into a school, after which the number of pupils grew rapidly. This is how the college was described round about the time that Joseph became a pupil there:

> [There are] ten commodious classrooms on the ground floor; beneath them are three large play-rooms, which are found extremely useful in wet weather. Above the classrooms come the dormitories, lofty and well lighted, and fitted with wooden partitions and curtains. There are, in addition, the refectory, a study hall – a place for class preparation, and fitted up with a handsome stage. Flanking this latter room is the domestic chapel [...] The gymnasium and bath are connected with the main building by a covered way [...] It is supplied by a well in the grounds, and is heated by steam. Swimming, we are glad to say, is encouraged. A boy, before being allowed to boat, must be able to swim four times the length of the bath in shirt, trousers, shoes and stockings. The gymnasium is under the care of a sergeant, who also has the task of drilling the students. There are also, as in every public school, other buildings devoted to workshops, laundry, dairy, and other erections connected with the farm and gardens.

Normally, a boy would stay at Beaumont for seven years, starting at the age of 11 or 12. Joseph, of course, had been sent to St Augustine's when he was 12 and had moved to Beaumont in 1885, shortly after his 15th birthday, which means that it is unlikely that he was a student there for more than four years.

Each year's intake at Beaumont, rather than having a numerical designation (First Form, Second Form, etc.), was given a title. These harked back to the continental tradition and were called Elements (the lowest form), Figures, Rudiments, Grammar, Syntax, Poetry, and, the most senior year, Rhetoric. In addition to these, 'special regard is had for modern requirements. The college has its army classes. All the classes are taught by members of the Society – a priest or one who is in preparation for the priesthood.'

The routine at Beaumont was similar to that which would have been found at that time at any of the leading English public schools. The students rose at 6.30 a.m., with morning prayers and chapel at 7 a.m. Breakfast was at 7.30 a.m. and morning studies began at 8 a.m. First schools (lessons) started at 9.15 a.m., followed by a break ('recreation') before second schools at 11.15 a.m. Between 12.15 p.m. and 3 p.m. were studies, preparation, dinner and recreation, followed by more study and afternoon schools, then chapel and night studies until supper at 7.30 p.m., after which there was recreation until 8.45 p.m. It was bedtime then for the younger boys, but the senior classes were allowed to study until 10 p.m.

It was a busy, hardworking routine, but perhaps not as Spartan and rigorous as it sounds. Sport was not neglected: Beaumont had a particularly good reputation for its prowess at Association football and there were annual fixtures with army teams from Sandhurst and Windsor Castle. At cricket the college was not so successful, owing to 'the rival summer attractions of boating and tennis', although, it was commented, 'perhaps the Beaumont boys will see to this, for they can oftener get a good game of cricket than of boating and tennis later on in life.' (However true

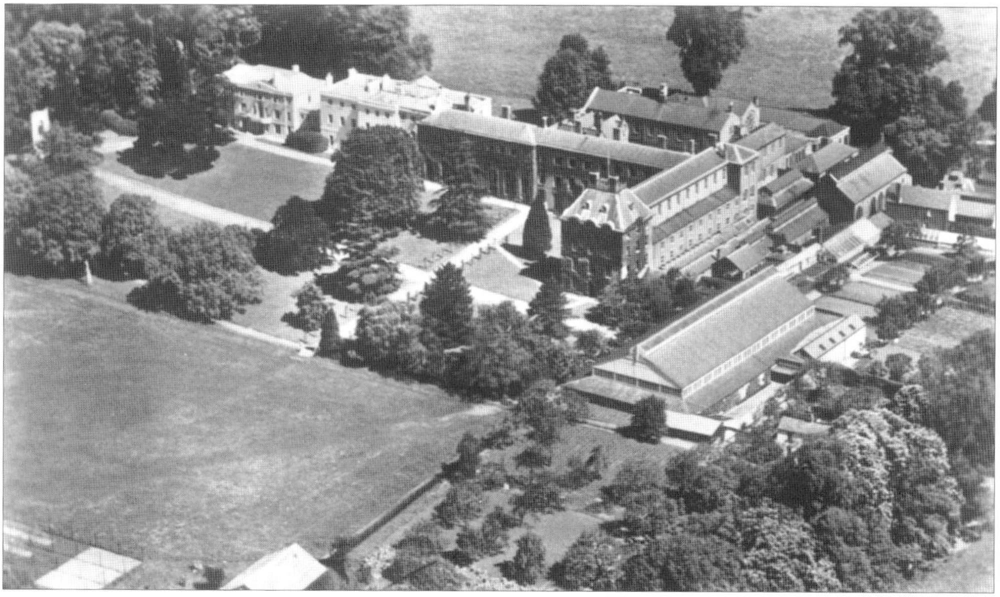

8 Beaumont College, Old Windsor

Joseph left St Augustine's in May 1885 and a few months later became a pupil at Beaumont College, Old Windsor. He was 15 years old. Beaumont was also a Catholic foundation, but otherwise was somewhat different from St Augustine's, not least in its geographical location. Instead of Ramsgate's windswept cliff top, Beaumont overlooked the Thames and was far from the sea. Often referred to as the 'Catholic Eton', it offered a typical English public-school curriculum, as well as the option of engaging in a wide range of sporting activities. Joseph left Beaumont in 1889 when he was 18 and enrolled in the National Art Training School in South Kensington, later to become the Royal College of Art.

9 *The cows in the meadow in the lower picture are there not merely to add picturesqueness to the scene: the College did indeed have its own farm.*

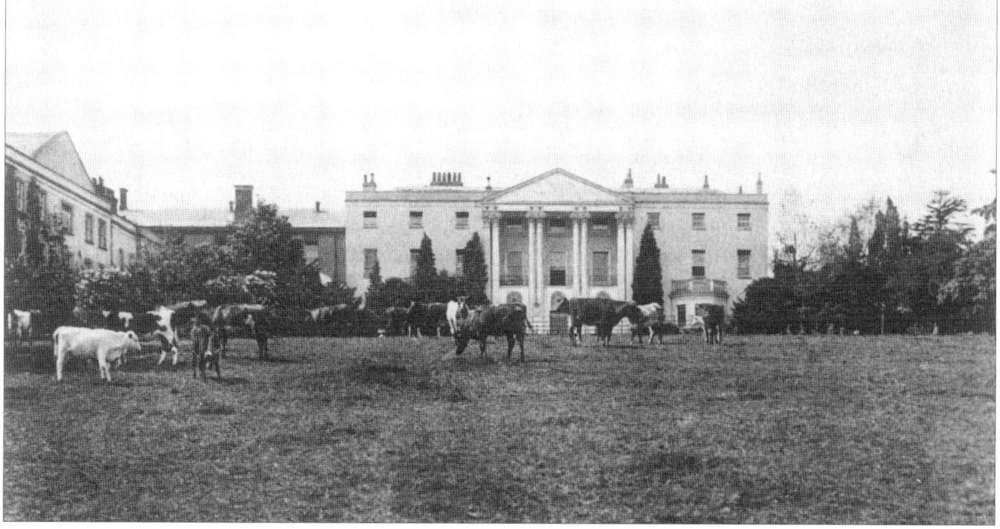

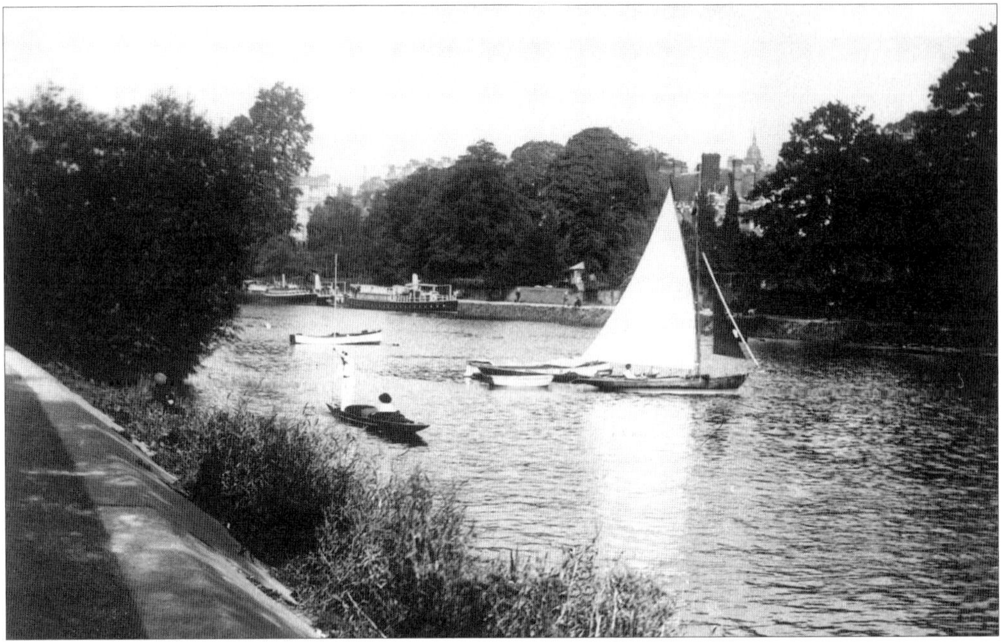

10 Boating on the Thames

Among the sporting activities permitted to the students at Beaumont College was boating. What the term 'boating' meant exactly is not known, but the college insisted that those choosing this sport be very competent swimmers before permission to take part was granted. Joseph Bagshawe was described later in life as having been a skilled yachtsman from an early age, but no indication is given as to how he acquired those skills. It is quite likely, however, that he sailed either on the Thames, which flowed close to the college, or on nearby Virginia Water. The postcard (above) is entitled: 'The Thames at Richmond' and shows a small yacht under sail such as Joseph might have practised in.

that might have been for the other students, it was certainly not to be so for Joseph, since, as we shall see, tennis was to play a major role in the courtship of his future wife, and he was also to become a passionate sailor and yachtsman.)

We do not know with certainty when Joseph left the college, although 1889 seems to be the most likely date. There is no reason to suppose that he was anything other than happy at school. He was certainly highly literate, not just in the sense of his command of the English language, grammar and syntax, but also in that, as his articles for various journals later were to show, he had the ability to write fluently, imaginatively, entertainingly and informatively. Moreover, his later published work is liberally sprinkled with foreign words and phrases, mainly French, but also Dutch, German, Latin and even the odd word or two in Russian. However, if one of the main, stated aims of Beaumont was to prepare its students for the university, in Joseph's case it failed in this objective – not, one suspects, because he was not bright enough, or that he was lazy, but, more likely, because by the time he left he had already decided upon his future calling: it was to become a professional artist.

Two

From South Kensington to North Yorkshire

On 7 March 1890, Joseph Bagshawe enlisted as a private soldier in the Artists' Rifles (or, to give them their full title, the 20th Middlesex Artists' Rifles Volunteer Corps), and swore the oath of allegiance to the Crown. It was a part-time, territorial unit that had been established 30 years earlier, in 1860, with its headquarters at Burlington House in Piccadilly. It was open to professional painters, sculptors, architects, engravers, musicians and actors. When Joseph joined, its honorary colonel was Sir Frederic Leighton (1830-96), President of the Royal Academy. (The regiment's linear successor today is the SAS.) What it was that prompted Joseph to enlist we can only guess. Perhaps his interest had been stimulated by the sergeant-instructor at Beaumont. Or it could have been a sense of patriotism in tune with the growing mood at that time of Britain's imperial destiny. More probably, he was attracted by the very title Artists' Rifles, since, after all, artist was his chosen profession. Or it may have been a combination of these factors, not to mention the appeal of camaraderie and summer camps.

That day, Joseph was duly inscribed on the muster roll; his regimental number was 3995 and he was allocated to C Company. It was recorded that he was 5 feet 11 inches in height, with a 35-inch chest, and was 19½ years old. His address was given as 249 Cromwell Road (his parents had by now moved from Hampstead to an even more substantial property in fashionable South Kensington), and, importantly for present purposes, his 'business' address was entered as the Art Training School, South Kensington.[1] It seems, therefore, that Joseph had gone directly from Beaumont College to art school, thus embarking upon a formal training as an artist (although, as we shall see, that training may have been somewhat limited).

There had been a Government School of Design since 1837, but it was the Great Exhibition of 1851 that provided a powerful boost to art training. Although the Exhibition had celebrated Britain's outstanding achievements in many fields, it also, it was argued, showed up 'her inferiority to the continental nations in the matter of artistic taste in her manufactures and in her industrial education policy'.[2] Consequently, the following year, 1852, the Privy Council set up a Department of Science and Art, the purpose of which was to provide popular instruction in the industrial arts, which in turn led to the creation of the National Art Training

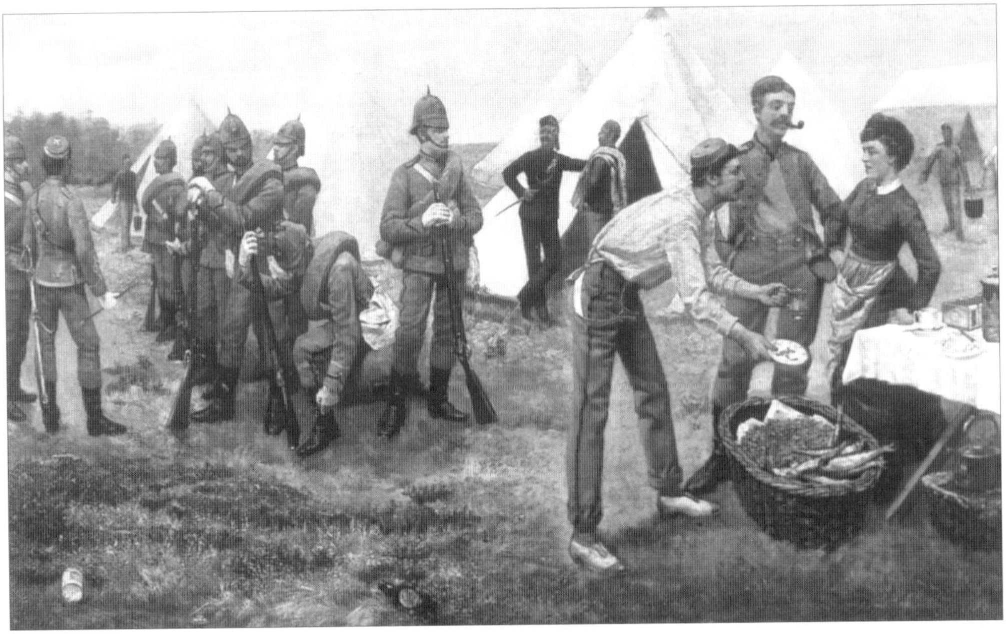

11 THE ARTISTS' RIFLES IN CAMP, 1884, BY GODFREY MERRY (FL. 1883-1915)

Joseph, having left Beaumont College in 1889 and the same year started to attend classes at the National Art Training School in South Kensington, a few months later, in March 1890, enlisted in the Artists' Rifles, a territorial unit made up of professional painters, sculptors, architects, engravers, musicians and actors. The regiment's honorary colonel at that time was Sir Frederic Leighton (1830-96), President of the Royal Academy. Whatever his motivation in taking this step – and camaraderie and summer camps may have been part of the attraction – it was a public statement of Joseph's commitment to his calling as an artist, although a possible sense of exclusiveness engendered by it may have had something to do with it, too.

Schools at South Kensington Museum (later, following the death of Prince Albert, to be known as the Victoria and Albert Museum).

From the outset, the Schools offered 20 subjects, with 60 subdivisions. Open to men and women alike, initially most instruction was provided separately. While the emphasis was on what might be termed the practical arts (design, technical drawing, architecture) and on training teachers who would themselves in turn go out into the schools and colleges to teach, there were also courses in various aspects of Fine Art (sketching, painting, perspective, drawing from life, the history of art). Indicative of the importance that the government attached to raising standards of art and design nationally were the financial resources invested in training: the South Kensington Schools were soon followed by the establishment of well over a hundred art training schools in all the most important towns and cities of the kingdom – it was estimated that, by the early 1880s, at least 300,000 persons were studying art in one form or another, whereas before the establishment of the South Kensington Schools fewer than 1,000 students annually were so engaged.

Admission to the Schools was relatively easy. There were, of course, tests to be taken and work to be submitted; but, given reasonable evidence of competence, the applicant would be accepted. There were evening courses as well as day courses; short-term courses as well as longer-term programmes. Fees were moderate and there were reductions for what were described as 'artisan' students, presumably men and women from less well-off backgrounds who worked during the day. Any student who presented drawings, paintings and models, who satisfactorily wrote papers on various art topics and who passed 'rigid and thorough' examinations would at the end of four years be awarded a diploma, which, it was proclaimed, is 'accepted throughout the civilised world as the highest award of excellence'.

Joseph served in the Artists' Rifles for a little over four years, resigning from the regiment in October 1894, which on the face of it suggests that he might have completed the full four-year course at South Kensington. On the other hand, thorough searches at the National Art Library have yielded no record of his having been awarded the diploma. Still, there is no doubt but that Joseph *did* attend in one capacity or another. Not only is there the evidence of the entry in the Artists' Rifles muster roll, but also that of the valedictory eulogy written shortly after his death by his friend and fellow artist, Hirst Walker, who stated that Bagshawe 'trained in art at South Kensington'.[3] However, his son, Wilfrid, writing, it is true, 24 years after his father's death, makes no reference to South Kensington, stating only that, following attendance at St Augustine's and Beaumont College, he 'thereafter studied art under Hubert Vos in London and afterwards under Van Hove in Bruges'.[4] But another scrap of evidence that he attended the National Art Training Schools in South Kensington is a surviving sketchbook (unfortunately undated) in the author's possession, inscribed in Bagshawe's hand:

J. Richard Bagshawe
N. A. T. Schools, S. Kensington
249, Cromwell Road, S.W.

Nonetheless, no document or diploma has been found to confirm that the full course of study was completed, which may suggest that although Joseph did indeed attend the Schools as an occasional day student, and may have audited certain lectures and practical drawing sessions (which would not have been difficult, living as he did at his parents' house in nearby Cromwell Road), he did not complete the full programme.

Another puzzle concerns exactly when Joseph studied under Vos and Van Hove: was it while he was studying at South Kensington, with the two activities overlapping each other, or was it after he left the Schools in or around 1894? It is known that Hubert Vos had opened a studio in London and lived there from 1885 to 1892, when he was appointed Holland's deputy commissioner for the Dutch exhibits at the Chicago World's Columbian Exposition,[5] which suggests that Joseph must have received tuition from him while at the same time attending classes at South Kensington, making it likely, therefore, that he went abroad to study with Van Hove in Bruges in 1894 (another source states that he studied at the Catholic University of Louvain, but provides no details to substantiate the claim).

Neither of the two artists mentioned could be remotely described as being a marine painter, although both hailed from the Low Countries, which have close associations with the sea. Vos was born in Maastricht in 1855 and studied at the Academy of Fine Arts in Brussels, and then in Paris and Rome. The recipient of several gold medals (Amsterdam, Munich, Dresden, Rome), in 1886 he was also honoured by the Salon des Artistes Francais for his painting *Ouvrir de l'Hospice de Bruxelles*. In general, he was known as a painter of genre scenes, portraits and as a *pasteliste*.[6] Similarly, Edmond Theodor Van Hove was born in Bruges in 1853 and is described as having been a painter of religious subjects, genre scenes and portraits. Among his works in public collections are *The Head of John the Baptist*, in Antwerp, and *The Botanist*, in Glasgow.[7]

It does not follow, of course, that because Bagshawe became a marine artist his teachers should have specialised in that genre, too. Very likely they offered instruction in various methods and techniques irrespective of their pupils' particular interests. Moreover, it is possible that they were chosen as much with an eye to religious considerations as to the purely artistic (especially since it would have been Joseph's father who paid the fees and supported his son financially).

A memoir[8] written by Joseph's wife after his death mentions that he studied art in Bruges for two years, which means he must have lived in Belgium from 1894 to 1896. Around that time he appears to have tried to establish himself as a writer and illustrator of occasional short stories.[9] One, entitled *The Sands of Kedreovet*, is described as being 'By J.R. Bagshawe, with illustrations by the author'. It tells the tale

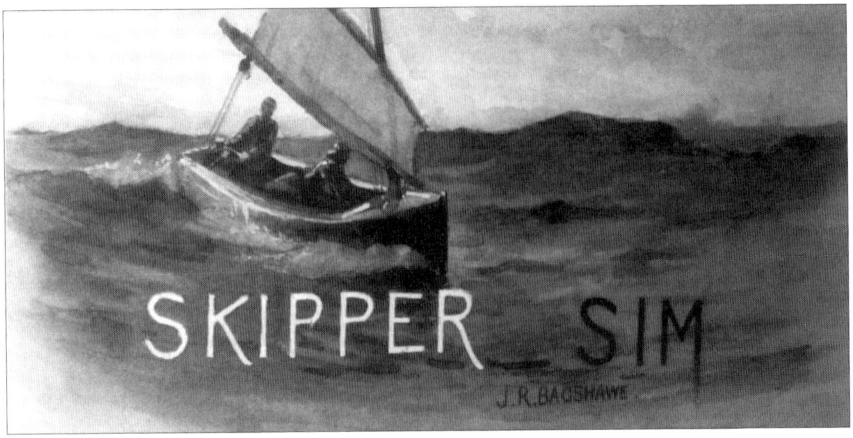

12 A Foray into Fiction: 'Skipper Sim'

In the early and mid-1890s, Joseph seems to have turned to illustration as an occasional source of income. Sometimes he illustrated short stories written by other authors; sometimes he was himself both author and illustrator. The quality of his fiction was, at best, indifferent; but his accompanying illustrations were already showing signs of the techniques that he would develop later in the decade. One piece, published in a penny magazine under the title 'Skipper Sim', tells a maudlin, typically Victorian tale of a young fisherman who sacrifices his own life in order to save that of a friend. Joseph's venture into fiction was apparently not a success, in contrast to his combining non-fictional prose and illustration towards the end of his life.

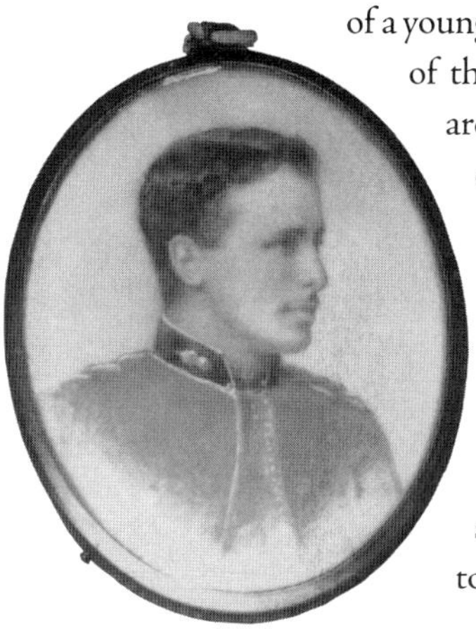

of a young Breton fisherman who drowns at sea and whose lover, on learning of this, throws herself into the waves and also perishes; their bodies are later washed ashore together. Then, in September 1896, Joseph did the illustrations for a tale published in the penny magazine *Short Stories* entitled 'The Singing Fishers'. It has a similar theme: a young fisherman is lost at sea, to be followed by his lover. More or less the same plot appears again in the same magazine the following year (8 May 1897) in a story about Skipper Sim, who sails on the lower Thames and the waters off Whitstable, Herne Bay and the North Foreland (an area familiar to Joseph from his schooldays in Ramsgate) and who sacrifices his own life in order to save that of a friend.

13 MAKING HIS WAY
Since leaving Beaumont in 1889, Joseph had lived with his parents at their home at 249 Cromwell Road in fashionable South Kensington. Following a period of study at the National Art School nearby, he spent two years, 1894 to 1896, in Belgium under the tutelage of Edmond Theodore Van Hove. Upon his return to London, Joseph seems to have entered upon a period of intense activity. He was awarded a prize by the South Kensington Sketching Club and in 1897 a fine miniature by him entitled The Right Honourable Viscount Southwell *was exhibited by the Society (later Royal Society) of Miniature Painters. At the same time, he was busy illustrating, and sometimes writing, short stories. That summer, 1897, for the first time, he had a painting hung at the Royal Academy's Summer Exhibition. Meanwhile, he had made his first visit to the Yorkshire coast.*

None of these stories displays much originality and Joseph's illustrations are of indifferent quality. However, 1898 finds his work appearing in a Catholic sixpenny magazine, *St Peter's*, accompanying a story by M.L. Handley entitled 'The Two Sides of the Door', and the following year sees the serialisation in the same publication of a novel, *The Hand of the Crusader*, by the Irish writer Katharine Tynan, for which Joseph provided all the illustrations.

Katharine Tynan (1861-1931) was an able, but not first-rank, author, who nonetheless played an important part in the literary awakening of modern Ireland: she was close to W.B. Yeats and his circle and herself published poetry, plays and over a hundred novels. She also concerned herself with social questions, notably children and working conditions for women, and thus, somewhat unusually for the time, combined Catholicism and feminism.[10]

As well as illustrating fiction, Joseph throughout this period was also busy painting more substantial work. Early on, he was awarded a prize by the South Kensington Sketching Club, and in Spring 1897 a meticulously painted miniature by him, entitled *The Right Honourable Viscount Southwell* (an Irish peer), was exhibited by the Society (later Royal Society) of Miniature Painters. It was said that the Society was so impressed that they urged Joseph to submit further work with a view to his being elected a member, but no more submissions were received. Perhaps this was because that same year, 1897, he had a picture hung, his first, in the Royal Academy's Summer Exhibition.[11] Entitled *Calm in the Channel,* it was described by a critic in *Punch* as a 'Delightful little picture. Might have been aptly called "Where all is Blue". There is no shore visible except in the name of the artist, J.R. Bagshawe, a grandson of that great marine painter, Clarkson Stanfield'. In the exhibition catalogue Joseph's address

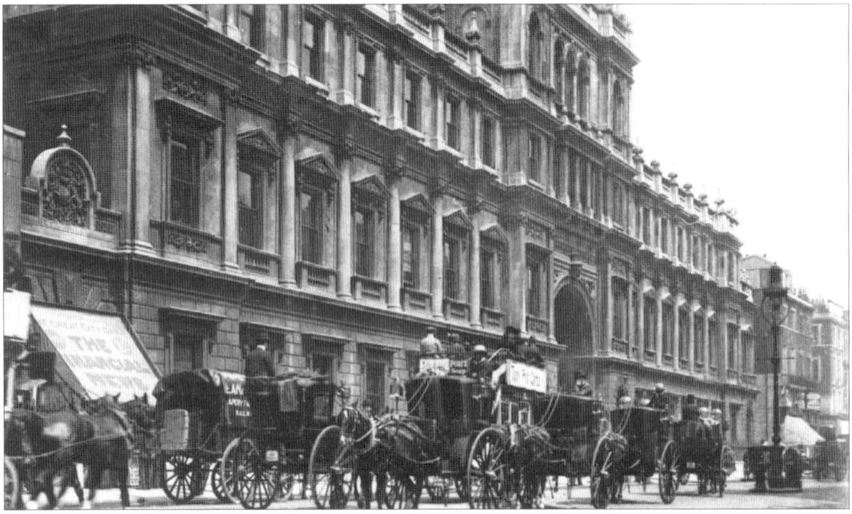

14 The Royal Academy of Arts, Burlington House, Piccadilly, London
The Royal Academy of Arts was founded by George III in 1768. Its first president was Joshua Reynolds, who was knighted the following year. Its imposing façade fronts onto Piccadilly (see above); beyond the archway is an inner courtyard surrounded by a number of learned societies. Forming one side of the square and directly facing the archway from within is the Royal Academy of Arts. It was here in 1897 that Joseph first had a painting selected (Calm in the Channel) *for hanging in the Academy's Summer Exhibition.*

is given as 4 Margravine Gardens, West Kensington, one of a pair of purpose-built artists' studios (although it is possible that he rented this solely for painting while continuing to live with his parents in Cromwell Road).

So far as is known, *Calm in the Channel* has not survived, but what is noticeable about Joseph's illustrative work in the years between 1896 and 1899 is that it appears to be evolving from a rather awkward, uncertain style towards one that is more fluid and impressionistic and one wonders whether something had happened to encourage the transition.

* * *

What it was that prompted Judge Bagshawe to choose Whitby on the North Yorkshire coast for his family's annual summer holiday in 1896 remains a mystery. The 'List of Visitors', a supplement to the weekly newspaper *The Whitby Gazette* (28 August 1896), announced that the Judge, Mrs Bagshawe and Family were staying at No.1 Mulgrave Place (in subsequent years they took No.3), a tall, terraced house at the seaward end of Skinner Street, 'dull, respectable Skinner Street', as one writer described it.[12] There was nothing to link the Bagshawe family with Whitby, although the resort had a favourable reputation for its quaintness and beauty, as well as being renowned for its bracing sea air, spectacular cliff scenery and the numerous picturesque walks in the vicinity. It was famed as the place where the Synod of Whitby (A.D. 664) had been held, which had settled the method for calculating the date of Easter, while the Venerable Bede dwells upon the wisdom and spirituality of the Abbess Hilda and recounts also the story of humble Caedmon, often referred to as the father of English verse. In the 18th century, Whitby had been a leading shipbuilding centre, a reputation greatly enhanced by Captain James Cook's having begun his career as a seaman in Whitby-built, Whitby-owned ships: later, having been commanded by the Admiralty to convey a group of scientists to the southern ocean in order to observe the passage of Venus, he chose, as he did for subsequent voyages of exploration, former Whitby colliers because of their robustness and construction (he must have often blessed their ability to 'sit the ground' whenever he fetched up on a remote shore many thousands of miles from home).

Mrs Gaskell was one of the literary luminaries who chose Whitby as their preferred resort in the 19th century: she began *Sylvia's Lovers*, her novel about the press gang's activities in Whitby (thinly disguised as Monkshaven), while lodging at

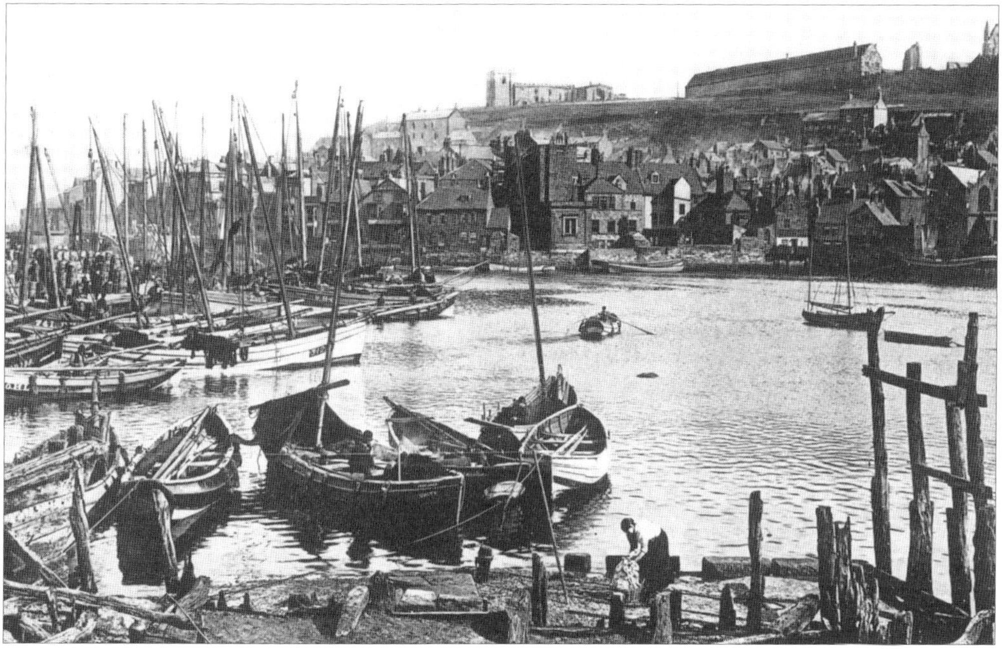

15 Whitby, North Yorkshire

Joseph first visited the ancient port and seaside resort of Whitby in 1896. As he emerged from the railway station, this is the scene that would have confronted him.

The upper harbour crowded with fishing boats (it was the herring season), while high on the cliff-top skyline was St Mary's parish church. Just visible (upper right) are the ruins of Whitby Abbey, a reminder of the town's famed ecclesiastical history. It was Whitby where James Cook had been apprenticed to a local ship-owner, who lived in one of the houses fronting the harbour slightly to the right of the centre of the picture. All the ships employed by Cook on his voyages of discovery were Whitby-built, including the most famous of them all, Endeavour.

Whitby was a favourite destination for many distinguished writers and artists, including Mrs Gaskell, Charles Dickens, John Ruskin, James Russell Lowell, Bram Stoker and C.L. Dodgson.

Judge Bagshawe and his family were to holiday in Whitby for several summers, renting rooms in a large house on the West Cliff.

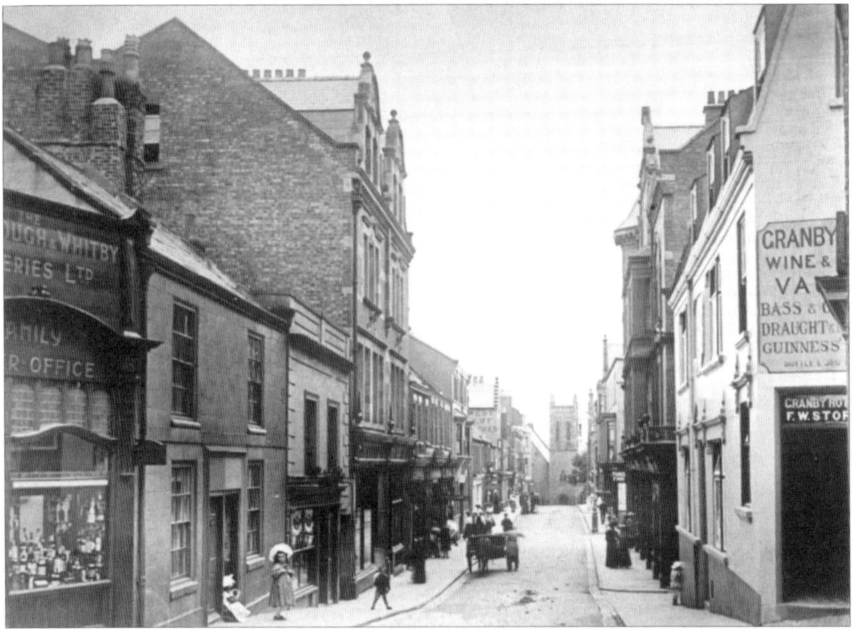

16 'DULL, RESPECTABLE SKINNER STREET'

That summer of 1896 the Bagshawes rented rooms at 1 Mulgrave Place, one of a short terrace of tall houses at the upper, seaward end of Skinner Street, 'dull, respectable Skinner Street', as one local writer dubbed it. In subsequent years they occupied an apartment at No. 3, which, through a gap in the street opposite, afforded them a splendid view of the Abbey on the East Cliff. Generally speaking, by this time, that part of the town that lay across the bridge on the east side of the River Esk was the poorer quarter, while the West Cliff side was more fashionable, having been developed largely as a result of the entrepreneurship of George Hudson, the so-called 'Railway King'.

It was on that holiday in 1896 that Joseph first met the young woman who was to become his wife, although it was to be another two years before they met again.

1 Abbey Terrace in 1859. But there were many others: Charles Dickens was a visitor, so was John Ruskin, while James Russell Lowell, poet and United States ambassador to the Court of St James, for many years stayed each summer with the Misses Galilee at 5 Wellington Terrace, just round the corner from Mulgrave Place.[13]

On 18 August 1887, Lowell wrote to a Miss Sedgewick in London:

> I am really at Whitby, whither I have been every summer but '85 for the last six years. This will tell you how much I like it. A very primitive place it is, and the manners and ways of its people much like those of New England [...] Tis a wonderfully picturesque place, with the bleaching bones of its Abbey standing aloof on the bluff, and dominating the country for leagues. Once, they say, the monks were lords as far as they could see. [...] Sea and moor, hill and dale; sea dotted with purple sails and white (fancy mixes a little in the purple perhaps), moors flushed with heather in blossom, and fields yellow with corn ... [...] I wish you could see the 'yards' – steep flights of stone steps hurrying down from the West cliff and the East, between which the river (whose name I never can remember) crawls into the sea [...] And I wish you could see the pier, with its throng of long-booted fishermen, looking the worthy descendants of the Northmen who first rowed their ships into the shelter of the cliffs, and named the place.[14]

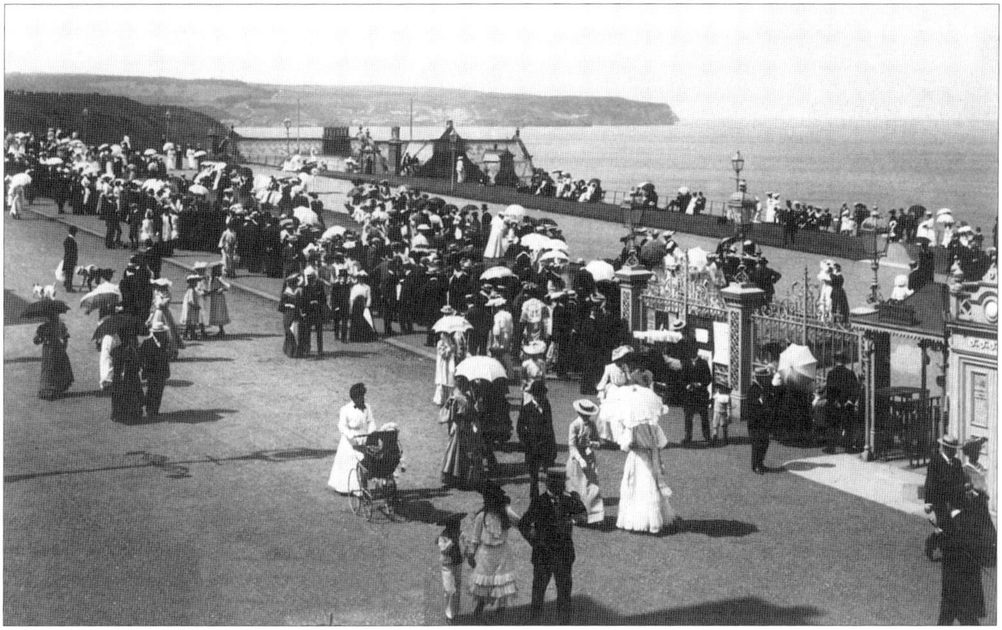

17 Beside the Sea

It was but a short walk from the Bagshawes' apartment in Mulgrave Place to the fashionable West Cliff Promenade. It was here that those well-to-do visitors who wished to see and be seen strolled in their finery. Everyone, children included, wore a hat, while many women carried a parasol – in those late Victorian and Edwardian days a pale complexion was more to be desired than a tan.

In the background, Sandsend Ness juts out into the North Sea, while in the bottom right-hand corner is the entrance to the Spa grounds, where a bandstand was situated. On the sands below there were more popular forms of entertainment, especially for the day-trippers who poured into Whitby by train during the summer months, escaping briefly from the industrial cities of West Yorkshire. As well as sea bathing (the bathing machines in the background bespeak a more modest age), there were also the pierrots. Again, sartorial niceties were observed: everyone wore a hat and no-one exposed their bodies to the sun.

18 *The sands at Whitby.*

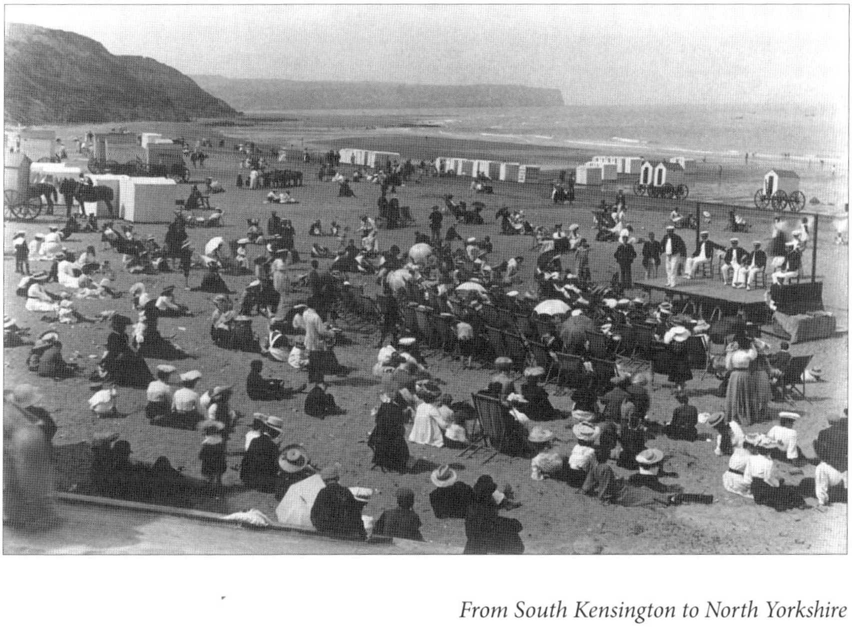

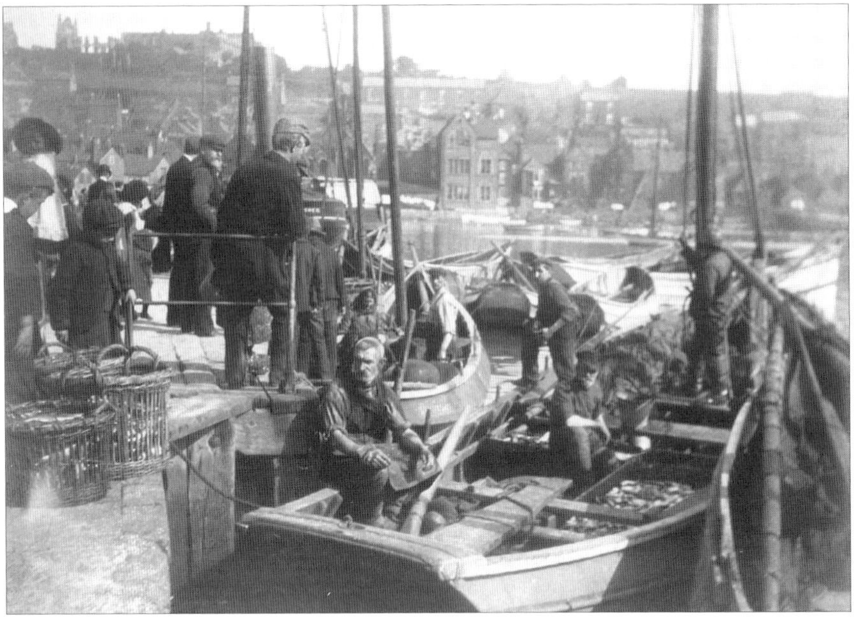

19 Fishing Boats

A major focus of interest for locals and visitors alike were the activities of the fishing fleet, particularly in August and September when the harbour was crowded with herring boats from all corners of the United Kingdom. In this photograph, taken, it is thought, by an amateur photographer, Greystone Bird of Bath, at about the time the Bagshawes visited Whitby, a large traditional, Yorkshire herring 'plosher' is moored alongside the quay in the upper harbour; the cribs are full of fish and the men are taking a break while waiting for their turn to unload the catch. Such scenes must have been of intense interest to Joseph, given his passion for the sea.

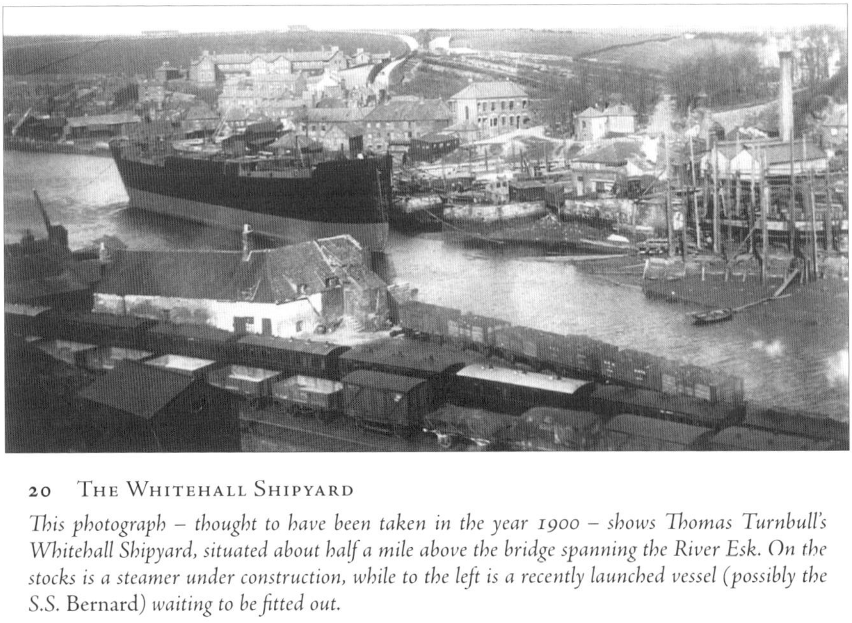

20 The Whitehall Shipyard

This photograph – thought to have been taken in the year 1900 – shows Thomas Turnbull's Whitehall Shipyard, situated about half a mile above the bridge spanning the River Esk. On the stocks is a steamer under construction, while to the left is a recently launched vessel (possibly the S.S. Bernard*) waiting to be fitted out.*

Bram Stoker was another writer who made Whitby his holiday destination: its ancient parish church on the East Cliff became the setting for the opening of his Gothic novel *Dracula*, while George Du Maurier and his family, and their large St Bernard dog, came every summer for many years – Lowell's 'long-booted fishermen' featured frequently in Du Maurier's cartoons for *Punch* (except that he called them the 'Vikings' of Whitby). And there were still more: John Leech, Henry James, Henry Irving, Edward Burne Jones, and C.L. Dodgson (better known as Lewis Carroll), who, it is said, was so inspired by the sweep of the sands between Whitby and Sandsend that he wrote the famous lines:

The Walrus and the Carpenter
Were walking close at hand,
They wept like anything to see
Such multitudes of sand.
'If this were only cleared away', they said,
'It would be grand!'
'If seven maids with seven mops
Swept it for half a year,
Do you suppose' the Walrus said,
'That they could get it clear?'

There was plenty to amuse and occupy the Bagshawes in Whitby. From their lodgings they could walk along Esplanade to the West Cliff Saloon to listen to the orchestra, or stroll along the Promenade, as so many visitors did, simply to see or be seen. There was the busy activity of the harbour, too, with boats unloading their catches or setting sail for the fishing grounds. Or they could hire a boat at nearby Ruswarp and row upstream to the Tea Gardens at Sleights. Then there were the Marquis of Normanby's beautiful woods, in the depths of which were the ruins of Old Mulgrave Castle. Or they could make excursions to any of the numerous waterfalls and beauty spots that were favourite destinations for holidaymakers. And on Sundays, of course, there was church. For the Bagshawes this would mean attendance at St Mary's Roman Catholic Church at the foot of Brunswick Street and its junction with Bagdale, a terrace of elegant 18th-century houses, known to locals as 'Amen Corner' because of the number of places of worship clustered there.

At some point, the Bagshawes may have had their portraits taken by one of the many photographers catering for holidaymakers, possibly by Frank Meadow Sutcliffe, whose reputation extended far beyond Whitby and was known worldwide. One activity for which we have tangible evidence for that summer of 1896 is a photograph discovered recently that shows Judge and Mrs Bagshawe with several members of their family, including Joseph, being rowed in a pilot coble (the traditional fishing craft of the North East coast) to inspect a vessel on the stocks prior to its being launched. The place was the Whitehall Shipyard situated some half a mile upstream of Whitby bridge on the Esk (the river whose name Robert Lowell never could remember!).

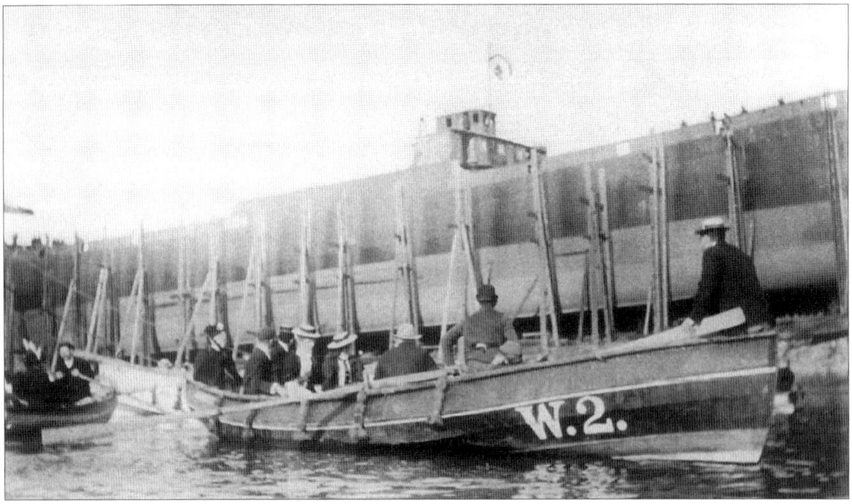

21 *The screw steamer* Alton *(5,150 tons) was the only vessel launched in the summer of 1896 from Thomas Turnbull's yard (the national economy was in recession). The Bagshawes and the Turnbulls were both Catholic families and it may have been this circumstance that initially brought Joseph and Mildred together socially. What is certain is that Judge Bagshawe hired a local fisherman to row his family upriver to inspect the* Alton *on the stocks just before she was launched.*

Mrs Bagshawe is seated in the stern of the boat, while Judge Bagshawe is amidships, next to the owner, who is wearing a dark-blue 'gansey' and a billycock hat. It is a traditional Yorkshire coble, although the registration W2 suggests that it was primarily a pilot boat (otherwise it would have been registered WY). The figure seated high in the bow is almost certainly Joseph.

Wooden sailing ships were no longer built at Whitby, wood having been replaced by iron in 1871, and later by steel. Trade was not good in 1896 and that year only two vessels left the slips.[15] Since the first, the *Glasgow*, was launched in February, and since the Bagshawes are lightly dressed, with Joseph wearing a straw boater, it must have been the second steamer, the *Alton* (the naming ceremony of which took place on 25 August) that the Bagshawes inspected.

It was during that holiday at Whitby in 1896 that Joseph and Mildred Turnbull, the only daughter of Thomas Turnbull, owner of the Whitehall Shipyard, first met. We do not know the circumstances, but it is quite likely that it was through the church. The Turnbulls, like the Bagshawes, were Catholics, so it may have been only a brief encounter occasioned by churchgoing. On the other hand, the two families occupied roughly the same social and economic position, so it is possible that the Turnbulls entertained the Bagshawes while they were staying in Whitby. Whatever the circumstances surrounding that first meeting, Mildred later recorded in her journal that it was to be another two years before they met again. Meanwhile, Joseph had discovered Staithes.

Three
Staithes

STAITHES IS A coastal village that lies to the north of Whitby. Until the late 19th century it was considered to be 'one of the most out-of-the-world spots to be found in England'.[1] The artist Nelly Erichsen was among the first to discover it and in an article published in *The English Illustrated Magazine* in 1886 she wrote:

> Down on the very edge of the North Sea, thrust out on rocky ledges, washed in winter by the salt foam, and climbing backwards up two steep headlands that tower above a brawling beck, lies a little fishing town [...] Invisible from the great northern highway, and, until last year, accessible only by the carrier's cart that dragged its weary weight over the twelve hilly miles from Whitby, this busy little town is little known to the outside world.[2]

It is a perfect description.

The very word 'staith' is of Scandinavian origin, which in turn is suggestive of early settlers, the Norsemen. As they ranged along the coast of what is now Yorkshire, they found few settlements between the Humber and the Tees, especially on the northern stretch beyond Streonshalh, which they renamed Whitby (the suffix '*by*' indicates Danish Viking settlement). What they were looking for was shelter for their boats, fresh water to drink, and space nearby on which to erect their dwellings. What they found was a tiny bay hemmed in by two rocky headlands, *nabs*, which, except when a gale blew from the north-east, afforded a modicum of protection against storms; a 'brawling beck'; and a narrow strip of relatively level land beneath the overhanging cliff. So, they set about shoring up this ribbon of land by driving in stakes to hold in place horizontal baulks of timber, before filling in any gaps with earth and boulders; in other words they built a staith, or quay, which in time gave its name to the place.

Staithes in 1817 was by far the most substantial fishing station on the Yorkshire coast. Out of 28 large yawls, 14 belonged to Staithes (whereas Scarborough, for example, had only three); while of the 250 smaller cobles, 70 fished out of Staithes.[3] Even as late as 1846 the historian John Walker Ord was able to report:

> The fishery at Staithes – especially in cod, haddocks and herring – is very important, being the main branch of commerce and the chief support of the place. Upwards of

> eighty boats, large and small, are in constant requisition during the season, the larger being manned by seven fishermen, the smaller four each, the remainder requiring only three hands. Upwards of three hundred men are engaged in this hazardous service, aided by numbers of women, who assist in collecting bait, mending the gear, and other necessary employments.[4]

However, by the last decades of the century the traditional pattern of fishing at Staithes (and elsewhere) was under threat, assailed by the advance of technology (especially trawling under steam) and the formation of a capitalist fishing industry centred on such ports as Hull and Grimsby. These were pressures that the individualistic, share-owning, three-man crews were increasingly unable to resist.[5] Still, when Erichsen and other artists started to arrive in Staithes and set up their studios what charmed, excited and inspired them was a community of fishermen and women who still spoke a distinctive dialect that varied even from that of the farming folk of the countryside that stretched from the top of the cliffs above to the high moors beyond; who held to powerful superstitions; and whose dress was, even then, somewhat old-fashioned and anachronistic. It was a community locked

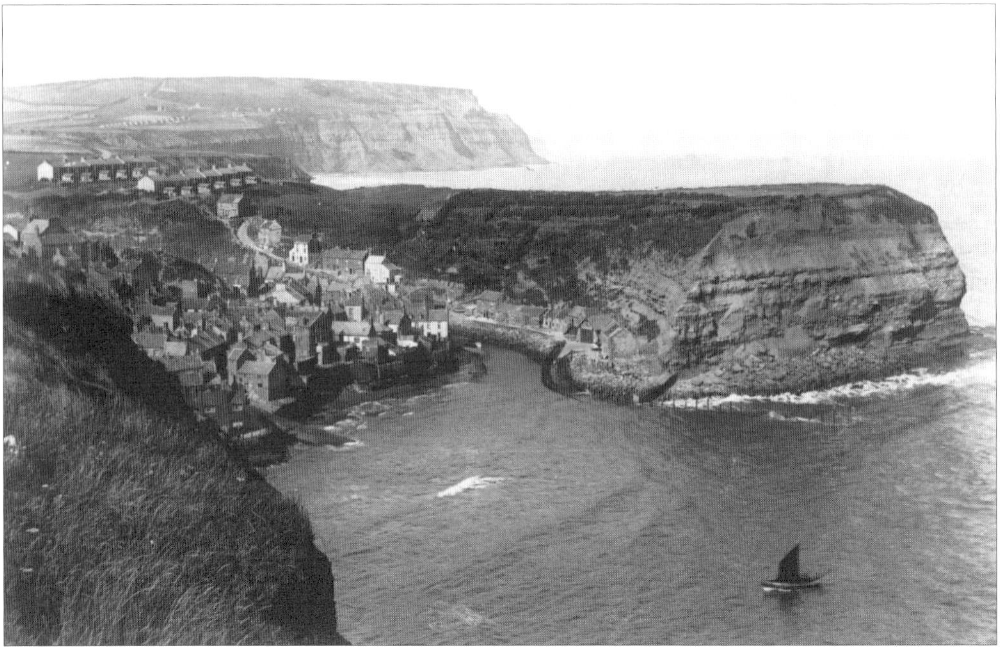

22 'A Little Fishing Town'

'Down on the edge of the North Sea, thrust out on rocky ledges, washed in winter by the salt foam, and climbing backwards up two steep headlands that tower above a brawling beck, lies a little fishing town.' (Nelly Erichsen, artist, 1886).

Boulby Cliffs (seen here in the background) are the highest in England. The bulk of Cowbar Nab offered some protection both for the village of Staithes and for the boats that sailed from off the open beach. The mouth of the 'brawling beck' is visible at the centre of the picture, with the fisherfolk's houses built out of the shore itself. The two terraces above the village were occupied by ironstone miners. The small craft (bottom right) is a Yorkshire coble and is approaching the land on a calm sea.

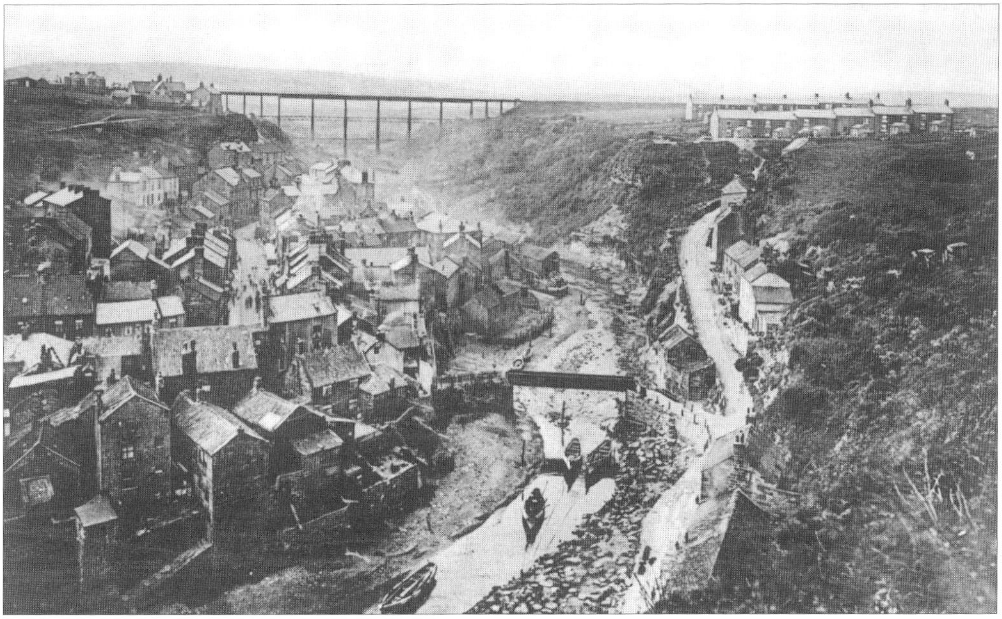

23 A VIEW OF STAITHES FROM COWBAR NAB LOOKING INLAND

This photograph (from a Frith postcard) gives a clearer impression of the huddle of houses and of the beck where several cobles are moored (a common practice when bad weather threatened). The miners' houses are top right, while in the background is the spectacular iron viaduct, opened in 1883, carrying the Whitby to Middlesbrough railway across the deep ravine. The railway not only stimulated tourists to visit the village, it also made the marketing of fish easier.

in a mighty struggle against the elements. Moreover, whereas the rural England of nostalgic memory was rapidly disappearing and being replaced by factories, mills, mines and expanding towns, here in Staithes could still be found a kind of peasantry, albeit of the seagoing variety, that had all but disappeared elsewhere.

The artistic preoccupation with the peasant had started in the mid-19th century in France when, in reaction to the stifling conventions imposed by the Parisian academic establishment, a number of painters moved to the village of Barbizon on the outskirts of the forest of Fontainebleau where they took as their subjects the simple peasant folk at their seasonal toil. Jean-Francois Millet (1814-75), Theodore Rousseau (1812-67), Charles Daubigny (1817-78) and Jean-Baptiste-Camille Corot (1796-1875) formed the core of this community, who all, directly or indirectly, followed a path trodden earlier by the English landscape painter John Constable (1776-1837). What distinguished them was not only their subject matter, but also their seeking to capture the light and colour of what they saw by painting out of doors, *en plein air*; their pioneering work was in turn to influence the impatient, radical young artists of the 1870s and 1880s, the French Impressionists. Painting *en plein air*, choosing as subjects peasants going about their daily pursuits, and an emphasis upon light and colour were all ideas that found favour with the artists who gathered in Staithes and in the neighbouring villages of Hinderwell and

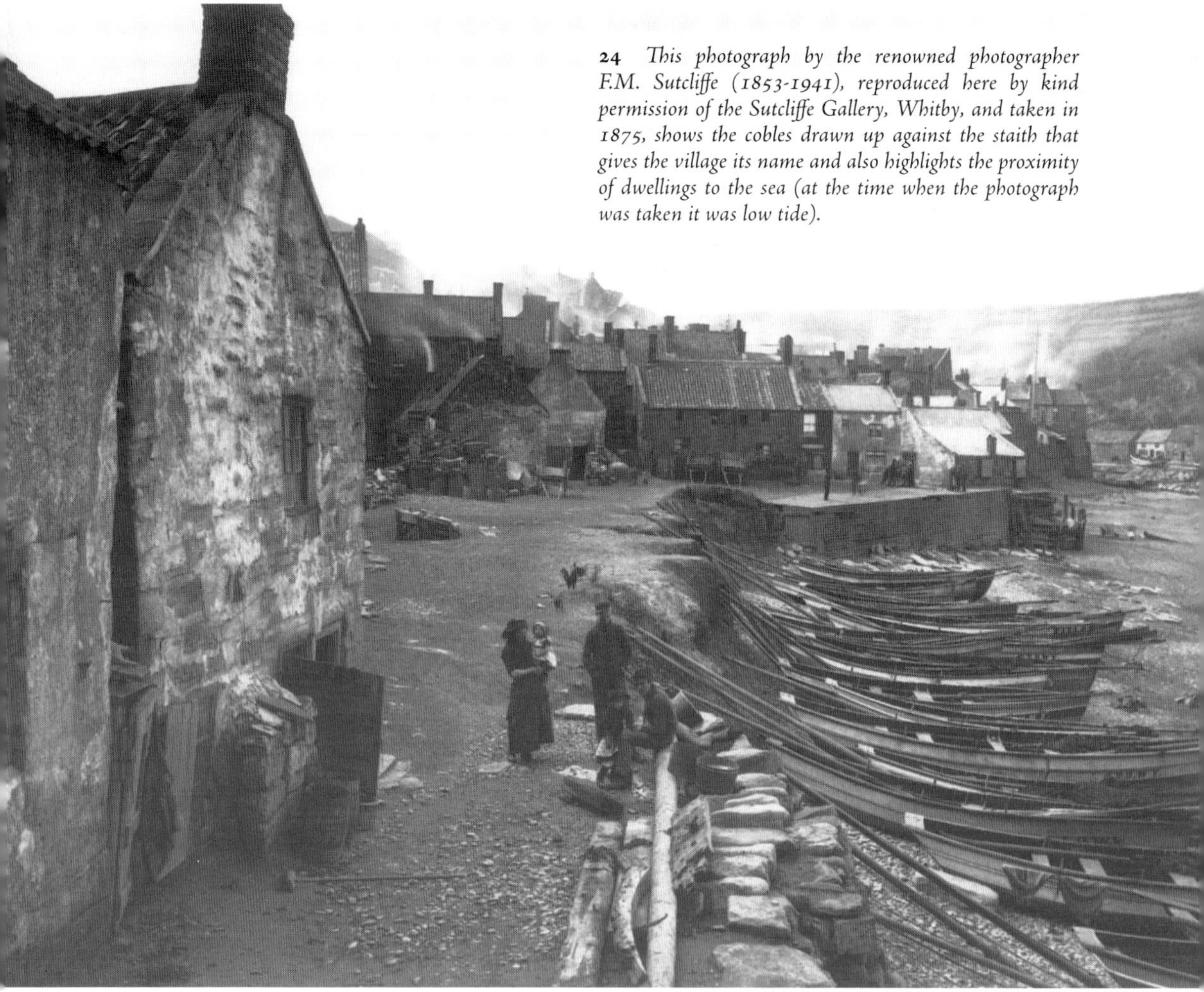

24 *This photograph by the renowned photographer F.M. Sutcliffe (1853-1941), reproduced here by kind permission of the Sutcliffe Gallery, Whitby, and taken in 1875, shows the cobles drawn up against the staith that gives the village its name and also highlights the proximity of dwellings to the sea (at the time when the photograph was taken it was low tide).*

Runswick Bay from the 1880s onwards, amongst whom were Laura Knight (*née* Johnson), her husband Harold, and Joseph Bagshawe.

One day in 1896, Laura happened to meet in the street Thomas Barratt, a Nottingham art master, who told her 'Staithes is the place to go! There is no place like it on all the coast for painting', whereupon with her aunt, and a friend, Rosie Good, she set off for the Yorkshire coast for a summer painting holiday. For Laura, it was like plunging into a 'whirlpool': 'The life of the fisher-people, the village itself, rocks and sea; impossible to know where to begin. You could not turn your head without seeing something you wanted to put on canvas – here was material for a landscape painter, a sea painter, a figure painter.' She reflected later:

> The life and place were what I had yearned for – the freedom, the austerity, the savagery, the wildness. I loved it passionately, over-whelmingly. I loved the cold and the northerly storms when no covering would protect you. I loved the strange race of

> people who lived there, whose stern, almost forbidding exterior formed such contrast to the warmth and richness of their natures.
>
> It bordered on the theatrical. There was every range of colour and intensity of light and dark, from the shadowy crowded alleyway to the spread of the sea [...] Its life ranged from the highest pitch of spiritual ecstasy to the depths of sordid tragedy. There was no such village on all the English shores – a place and a people apart.[6]

In the same year, 1896, that Laura Johnson was spending her summer holiday in Staithes, Joseph Bagshawe was spending his at nearby Whitby. It is quite likely that he had heard of Staithes and its colony of artists already. Being London-based and an aspiring artist himself he would doubtless when visiting the Royal Academy's summer exhibitions have seen there works by painters such as Mark Senior, Ernest Dade, Arthur Friedenson, Fred Jackson and others. Then there were the art magazines that from time to time carried articles about Staithes and Runswick. And even if by remote chance he did not know about the Staithes artists before his visit to Whitby, he would surely hear about them during his stay – there was, for instance, Anderson's gallery just round the corner from the Bagshawe family's lodgings, where local painters' work was displayed for sale. But nothing could have prepared him for Staithes itself. It seems to have seized him, captivated him, fascinated him, inspired him: henceforth, to the end of his days, it was to be the passionate focus of his artistic activity.

The effect of Staithes upon Joseph bears some resemblance to that of Cullercoats, a fishing village near the mouth of the Tyne, upon the famed American painter Winslow Homer, shortly after his arrival in England in 1881. Homer already had an established reputation as an artist and was known principally for his depiction of the American Civil War and for scenes of domestic rural life. It was noticed that the figure of a young woman featured in several of his paintings, most noticeably in *Blackboard* (National Gallery of Art, Washington, D.C., 1877). Then the young woman disappeared from his work, and Homer himself began to withdraw from friends and society, so that, by 1881, it was said that he had retired 'wholly within himself' into 'grim and misanthropic seclusion'.[7] Some critics have concluded that this behaviour was evidence that he had been rejected and that he was thwarted in his love for the young woman and that that is why he left America for England. Be that as it may, as a result of his stay on the Northumberland coast,

> Homer suddenly and categorically refashioned his art. Instead of the pastimes of young people at school or at the seaside that he depicted in his American paintings, his English watercolours illustrate older people, their figures ampler and weightier, their transactions with nature more insistently serious and sometimes perilous. The changes in Homer's art that first appeared in his English watercolours assume more monumental form and almost tragic significance in a series of large, heroic oils that he painted in the years immediately following his return to America. There is no precedent in Homer's earlier art for the subject, scale, or the gravity of meaning of a work such as *The Fog Warning* [Museum of Fine Arts, Boston, USA, 1885].[8]

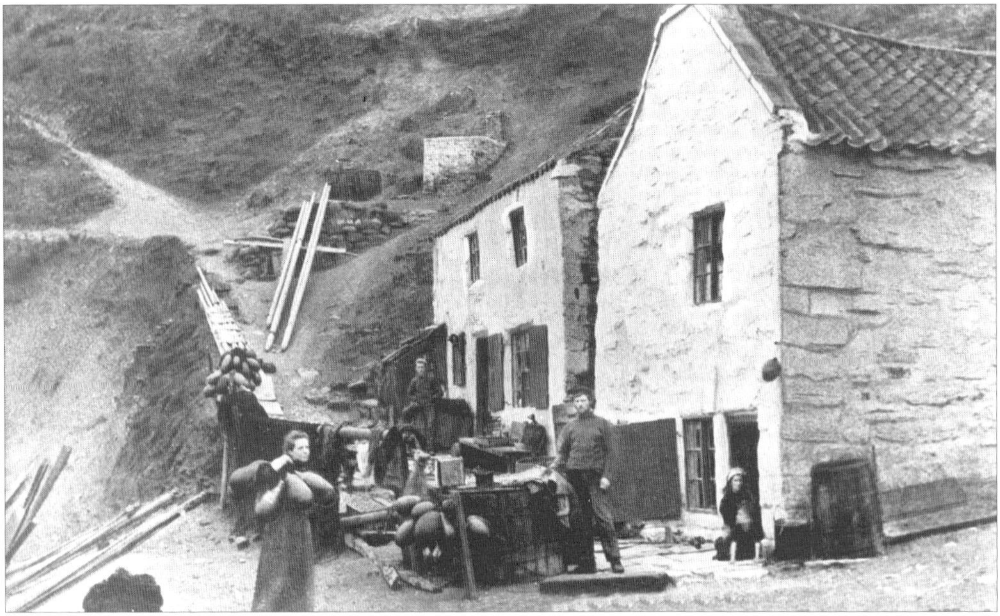

25 *The two dwellings depicted in the previous illustration are shown again here from the opposite side. Although in contrast to Sutcliffe's photograph this one is technically of poor quality, from a social history point of view it contains a great deal of detail. The woman in the doorway of the cottage on the right (wearing a bonnet) is standing below the level of the staith. Also, all the lower windows are shuttered. This is because in stormy weather the sea would break against the houses themselves (see next two illustrations). The man is resting his hand on a frame over which herring nets are drying. Attached to the nets are inflated tarred animal bladders used to give the nets buoyancy (the girl has a bunch over her shoulder and there are yet more laid out on the spars behind). Also arranged on the spars are split fish, usually a type known as blackjack, a kind of pollock, which were salted and dried in the open air for use during the winter. Part of the way up the cliff is a stone structure containing a copper in which cutch was heated and into which the nets were dipped to preserve them. The activities of the fisherfolk were an endless fascination for the artists who congregated at Staithes and none more so than Joseph Bagshawe.*

Not that Joseph Bagshawe was thwarted in love in that summer of 1896. Nor, unlike Homer, did he already have an established reputation as an artist, far from it; he was just beginning to make his way. But that something impacted upon him at around that time there can be little doubt. After 1896 he was a frequent visitor to the north-east coast of Yorkshire. He spent the entire winter of 1898-9 at Staithes, painting and sketching, and in 1901 he had two pictures hung at the Royal Academy's Summer Exhibition, *In Peril* and *Ebb Tide*, both featuring Staithes and the Yorkshire coble. In short, what is being suggested here is that Bagshawe, with his public-school, upper professional middle-class, metropolitan background, had discovered a community of fisherfolk clustered at the very edge of the sea, confronting the elements, experiencing tragedy and joy in the course of their toil, such as he had never witnessed before with such intensity, and that it was this that set the course for the rest of his artistic life.

Again unlike Homer, Joseph Bagshawe was no recluse; in fact, all accounts agree that he was a kindly man, gregarious, a good conversationalist, extremely courteous and excellent company, attributes that doubtless go a good way towards accounting for his wooing and winning the hand of Mildred Turnbull*, whom he had met briefly on his first visit to Whitby in 1896. They met again two years later.

Mildred Turnbull was the only daughter of Thomas Turnbull, ship-owner and ship-builder, and his wife Georgiana, and, as such, enjoyed a comfortable, privileged lifestyle. She was not obliged to work, nor did she. She lived at home with her parents, waited on by servants, in an imposing Georgian mansion, Airy Hill, built in 1790 by Richard Moorsom, father of Admiral Sir Robert Moorsom, who was to command one of Nelson's ships, the *Revenge*, at the battle of Trafalgar (in commemoration of which a sun dial made of bar-shot retrieved from *Revenge* after the battle stood on the south lawn and is now in Whitby Museum). The house, designed by Carr of York and built of stone from the nearby Eskdaleside quarries, was set in spacious grounds above the port, yet, as the crow flies, only a short distance across the river from Thomas Turnbull's yard.

By all accounts, Mildred was a dutiful, loving daughter, whose pastimes included walking, cycling, hockey and horse riding. Moreover, at a time when few women had access to higher educational institutions, she sat the Cambridge External Examination: the subject that year, 1895, was 'The Colonies'. 'I did pretty decently', she noted in her journal, 'and answered the nine questions and passed with "Distinction".'

Judging by her diaries, Mildred was a fun-loving young woman who enjoyed an active social life, albeit circumscribed by the manners and mores of the late Victorian age. She was pleasing, rather than beautiful, but her zest for life doubtless lent her added lustre. She appears to have had no shortage of eligible admirers, one of whom was a scion of another well-to-do Whitby ship-owning family. Recalling the events of Saturday 22 May 1895, she wrote in her diary:

> Christened Harold Smales' new yacht. *Gt* fun. They had a lovely christening cake which I was made to cut! The yacht is very pretty, and is called '*Janet*'!!* I have made a cushion for it.

Three months later, she noted:

> August 27th. Regatta. H. Smales won 1st prize in yacht race with the '*Janet*'.

And then, on 1 September:

> Ethel [presumably a friend or relation, and chaperone] and I went for a sail with H. in the '*Janet*'. [...] Went as far as Skinningrove [beyond Staithes, about fifteen miles up the coast] – great fun, plenty of wind but not rough. Had tea on board. Awfully pretty little yacht. I steered nearly all the time, under H's supervision, of course.

* Janet Mildred Alice Turnbull was known within the Turnbull family as Mildred. After her marriage, she was referred to as Janet by the Bagshawes, although a postcard sent by her husband Joseph from Bern in Switzerland and postmarked 19 November 1902 was addressed to Mrs Bagshawe, Airy Hill, Whitby, and began 'Dearest Mildred'.

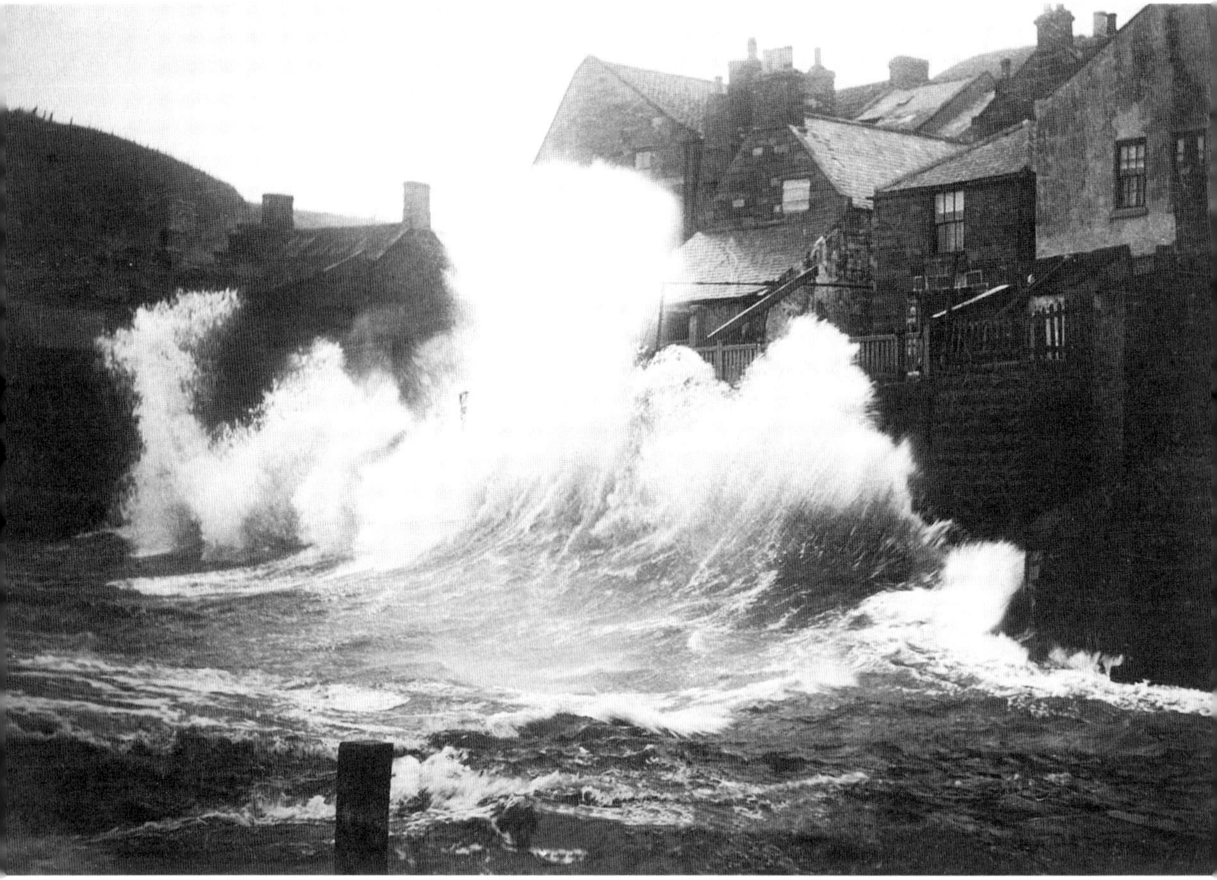

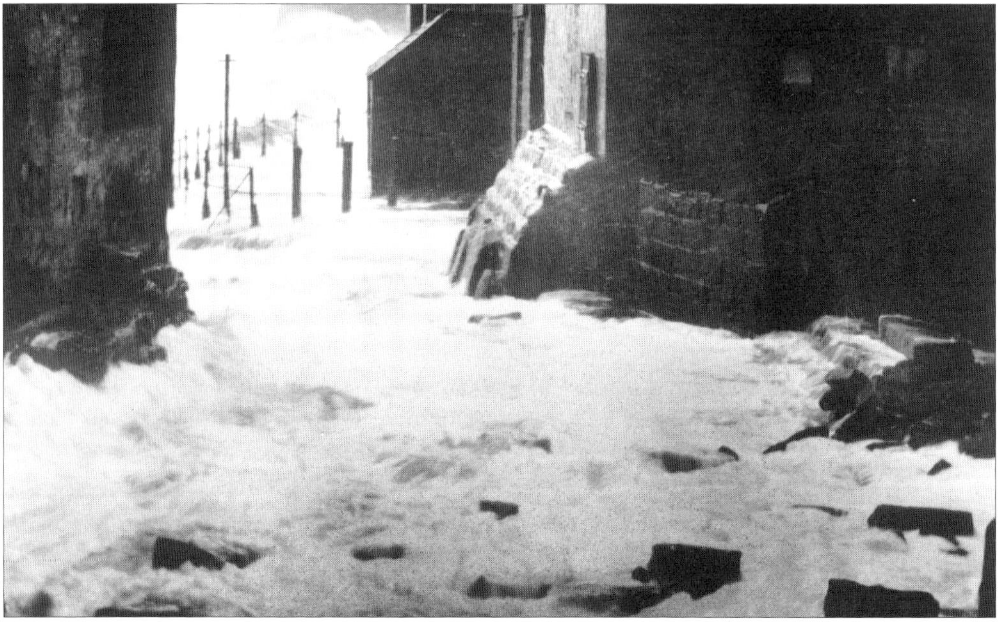

Harold makes one more appearance in Mildred's journal – in August 1898, when, on the 12th, a party of friends and acquaintances rode on their bicycles to Falling Foss, a noted beauty spot hidden away in woods not far from Whitby. There, in first place, were listed the Smaleses, followed by the Brotchies, the Hirsts, Miss Draper, H. Walker, Mr Williams and others. Then, apparently added later (almost as an afterthought, judging by the slightly different ink), comes the name 'J. Bagshawe'.

If that was Harold Smales's last appearance in Mildred's journal, it was certainly not J. Bagshawe's. Just five days later (17 August), the entry reads:

> Another bicycle picnic, to the Aislaby Moor this time. Didn't ask quite so many – had great fun, glorious day. Went to palmist Esmeralda in the evening. Mr Bagshawe told fortunes in the afternoon at our picnic.

The very next day, 18 August, Mildred, accompanied again by Miss Draper, played tennis all morning with J. Bagshawe (how wrong the Beaumont critics had been about the pointlessness of learning to play this game!). From that day forward, Joseph is mentioned constantly: picnic excursions by wagonette or carriage; more tennis; calls by Joseph and his sister Teresa (the family were again staying in Whitby) at Airy Hill. Then, on 14 September, Mildred wrote:

> Drove to Ellerbeck [a beauty spot on the Goathland moors] with the Bagshawes – glorious weather, great fun. Left at 11.30, got back at 8 p.m. Delightful walk up the stream – huge bunch of heather. [*Still* pinned to the journal beside this entry is a faded sprig of heather – it is not hard to guess who had plucked it and given it to Mildred as a *momento.*]

The day following the excursion to Ellerbeck, 15 September (the date is underlined), Mildred writes that she 'rode with Joe Bagshawe in the morning – splendid gallop on the sands'. This is the first time she refers to Joseph by his diminutive, Joe, and, it seems, the first time they go out together unaccompanied.

26 & 27 *(Facing page) The village of Staithes was built originally by squatters, fishing families who erected their dwellings on a narrow strip of land at the very edge of the sea itself. At the time when Joseph Bagshawe was active there, there were no breakwaters to moderate the force of the waves when storms raged.*

Steers (as locals pronounced Staithes) had

Hooses up yah spot
An' hooses down in another
An' t'great big sea weshing
Reet up tiv it.

– From Rhymes and Sketches to Illustrate the Cleveland Dialect *by C.M. Tweddle (1892), quoted by John Howard in his* Staithes: Chapters from the History of a Seafaring Town *(2000).*

Staithes

Were we to rely solely upon the evidence of Mildred's journals, it would appear that from that day she and Joseph enter upon a lengthy courtship that culminates on St Valentine's Day 1901, some two and a half years later, with the announcement of their engagement. However, in a memoir written after Joseph's death, Mildred reveals that she and Joe had in fact become engaged just *one month* after that first bicycle picnic to Falling Foss. Joe and I, she wrote,

> met August 1896, then not again till August 1898. Saw each other constantly – rode together, picnics, etc. [...] Became engaged September 15th [1898]. Rode next day by Dunsley to the sands.

Little wonder, then, that the date, 15 September, is heavily underlined in Mildred's journal, no wonder they rode out the next day for the first time unchaperoned. It had been a whirlwind romance and the start of a truly happy partnership.

From now on, Joseph divided his time between London and Yorkshire. During the first winter spent at Staithes in 1898-9 he observed the life of the village from within. He filled his notebooks with sketches of the fisherfolk going about

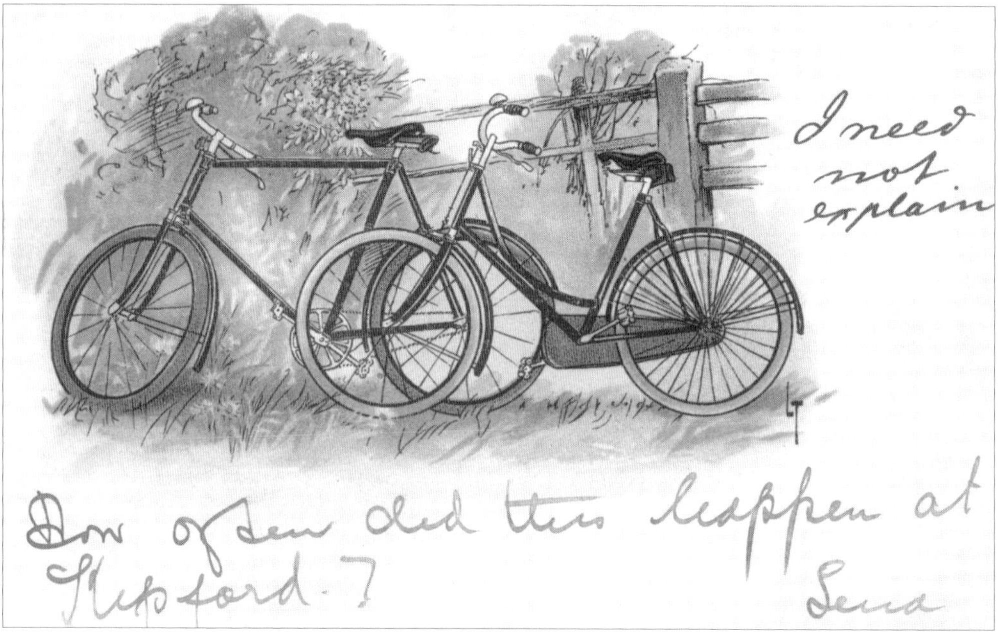

28 Second Meeting

Having met briefly in the summer of 1896, Joseph Bagshawe and Mildred Turnbull renewed their acquaintance two years later, in the summer of 1898, when the Bagshawes were again on holiday in Whitby. As it happens, the bicycle was to play a part in the romance that followed.

The invention of the safety bicycle had widespread social effects, not least for women, who thereby acquired a mobility largely denied to them previously. Patterns of courtship also changed and this postcard (dating from around 1900) by Lance Thackeray makes the point nicely. The woman's bicycle leans against the man's, yet the riders are nowhere to be seen (in the bushes?). 'I need not explain', runs the caption, while the sender writes to her friend, 'How often did this happen ...?'.

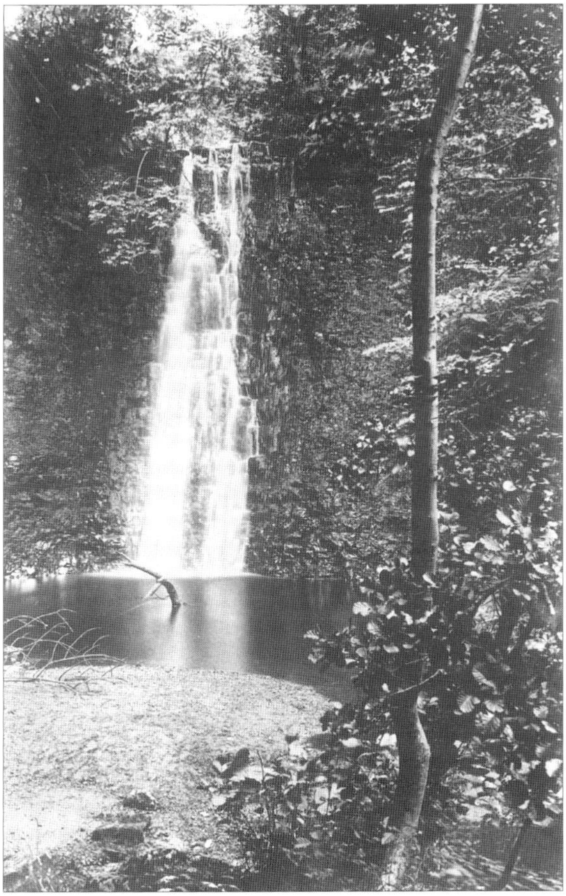

29 Bicycle Picnics

Mildred Turnbull was a sporty young woman, fond of hockey, horse-riding and cycling. On 12 August 1898, according to an entry in her journal, she arranged a cycling picnic for a group of friends to a local beauty spot, Falling Foss, a few miles from Whitby. This is how a contemporary guide book described it: 'Hidden away in the thickest part of a dense wood, the sound of the waterfall guides your feet and falls pleasantly on your ear before you can see it. [It] falls in myriads of crystalline particles. The out-of-the-way and romantic character of the place lends it an additional charm.'

This excursion was followed a few days later by another bicycle picnic, to which Joseph was again invited.

their business and the contours and characteristics of their boats. His biggest challenge was the Yorkshire coble, a craft that had evolved over many centuries. It is popularly believed to be descended from the longships, and, indeed, it shares many of the features of its Viking predecessors. However, whereas the longship originated in the deep fjords of Norway and Denmark, the north Yorkshire coast is fringed by rocky, shelving beaches that demand a largely flat-bottomed craft with a square, sloping stern that can be landed stern first and dragged above high-water mark during stormy weather. At the same time, the bow of the coble is sharp and deep, so that it cleaves the waves when launching from an open beach, and, finally, there is an unusually long rudder that projects well below the bottom of the boat, thus providing a degree of stability when under way. The lines of the coble look deceptively simple at first sight; in fact, they consist of subtle curves, the planks rising slightly at the stern, almost flat amidships, before gracefully sharpening at the bow; in cross section the coble has a pronounced 'tumblehome', so that, as one traditional coble builder put it, 'There is always a strake (plank) square on to the sea.'[9] Very few artists, then or now, get the coble right, but Joseph Bagshawe is one of them.

Joseph was not painting in isolation in Staithes. By 1898, a score or more artists had congregated there and in the neighbouring villages, exactly how many varying with the seasons. There was no formal group, no particular leader (although certain artists commanded special respect), no agreed principles, let alone an ideology – beyond, that is, a commitment to painting people and nature as they saw them, and, for many, working *en plein air*.

The Bagshawes continued to spend their summer holidays at Whitby each year, renting an apartment at 3 Mulgrave Place. Quite often, Joseph went 'up to town', sometimes to work up his sketches into paintings, sometimes for family reasons – for example, he returned home in February 1900 to bid farewell to his 21-year-old brother Edward, who was about to embark for the Transvaal with the 3rd Battalion The Princess of Wales's Own Yorkshire Regiment (he survived the Boer War, but was killed in action on the Somme on 22 July 1916). It is perhaps indicative of Joseph's preoccupation with his private life that, having had his painting *Calm in the Channel* selected for the Royal Academy's Summer Exhibition in 1897, he had to wait until 1900 before gaining further success with *Eve of the Storm*, *Her Last Signal* and *A Nor'wester*.

With the onset of the new century, the outlook for Joseph and Mildred must have seemed rosy. They were engaged, albeit without making their betrothal public; Joseph was an accepted member of the community of artists at Staithes, and his professional career was progressing well (by now, he had in all had five paintings accepted by the Royal Academy). Things were not so tranquil, however,

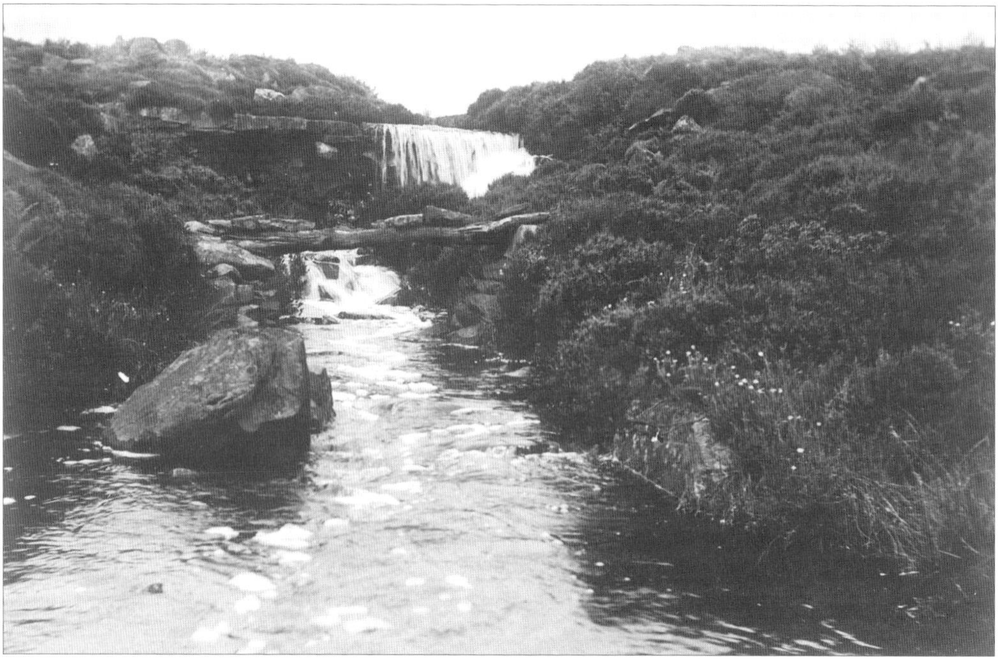

30 Ellerbeck – A Memorable Day

It was not long after the bicycle picnics that Joseph and Mildred's families came together and went on an excursion to a picturesque spot high on the moors between Whitby and Pickering. Here was a rushing, tumbling beck, the banks of which were covered in heather in full bloom. The date was 14 September 1898 and Mildred noted in her journal: 'Drove to Ellerbeck with the Bagshawes – glorious weather, great fun. Left at 11.30, got back at 8 p.m. Delightful walk up the stream – huge bunch of heather.' Still pinned to the page in Mildred's journal, more than a century later, is a faded sprig of heather, doubtless plucked and handed to her by Joseph that memorable day. Even more memorable, however, was the next day, 15 September, for that was the day that Joseph and Mildred became secretly engaged, just one month after that first bicycle picnic to Falling Foss.

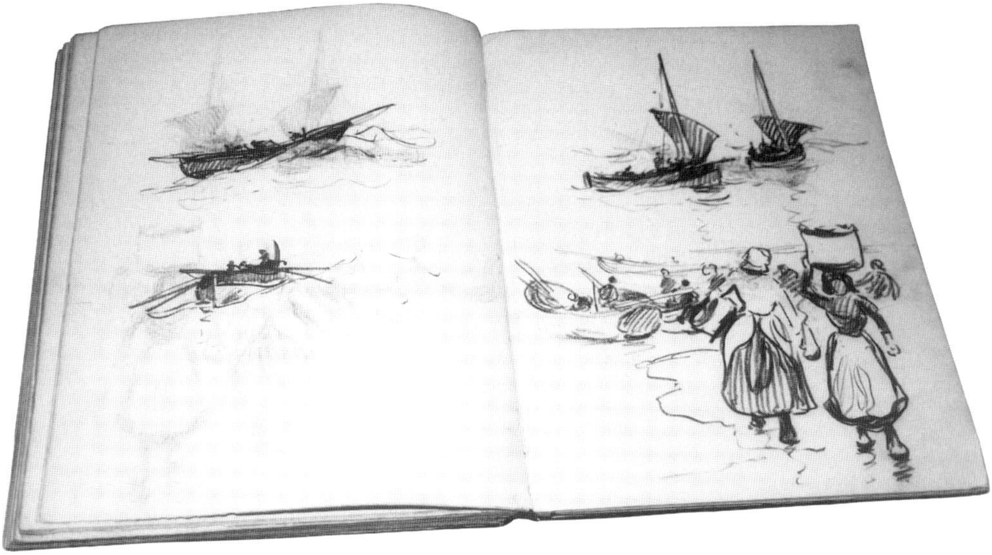

31 Staithes, Winter, 1898-9

It was probably a combination of his quiet engagement to Mildred and the attraction of the community and its artists that was the reason for Joseph's deciding to take lodgings in Staithes in the winter of 1898-9. Although henceforth he never completely severed his connections with London (his parents continued to live there), the main focus of his artistic activity became the North Yorkshire coast. That winter, Joseph busied himself by getting to know the fisherfolk and their ways, socialising with his fellow artists, and sketching and painting the life of the village. This is a page from his sketchbook. It illustrates his fascination for the Yorkshire coble (he was, and remains, one of very few artists who have caught accurately the features of that craft), and depicts the hardy women who were such an integral part of the inshore fishing economy.

in the country at large. There was turmoil in the political realm: Home Rule for Ireland, the rise of the Labour Party and the growing influence of the trade unions, and Women's Suffrage were all acutely controversial and divisive issues at the turn of the century. Queen Victoria, born in 1819, had come to the throne in 1837 at the age of 18, but she was now 81 and had reigned for 63 years: it was obvious that she could not continue for much longer and that a change of monarch was imminent (she died the following year, greatly mourned, but leaving a country hoping for a more relaxed reign). And Edward VII was indeed in many respects a refreshing contrast to his mother. He concerned himself more with ceremonial than with seeking to exercise political influence over government; he set new fashions; while his amorous liaisons (he is said to have had 13 mistresses – presumably not all at once! – many of them actresses) brought him notoriety and popularity in almost equal measure. His reign, 1901-9, was a period of very rapid social, political and technological change (for example, the motor car, the telephone and the aeroplane all came to the fore in these years). Yet the 'Edwardian era' was not always as jolly and gay as it is often depicted, for while

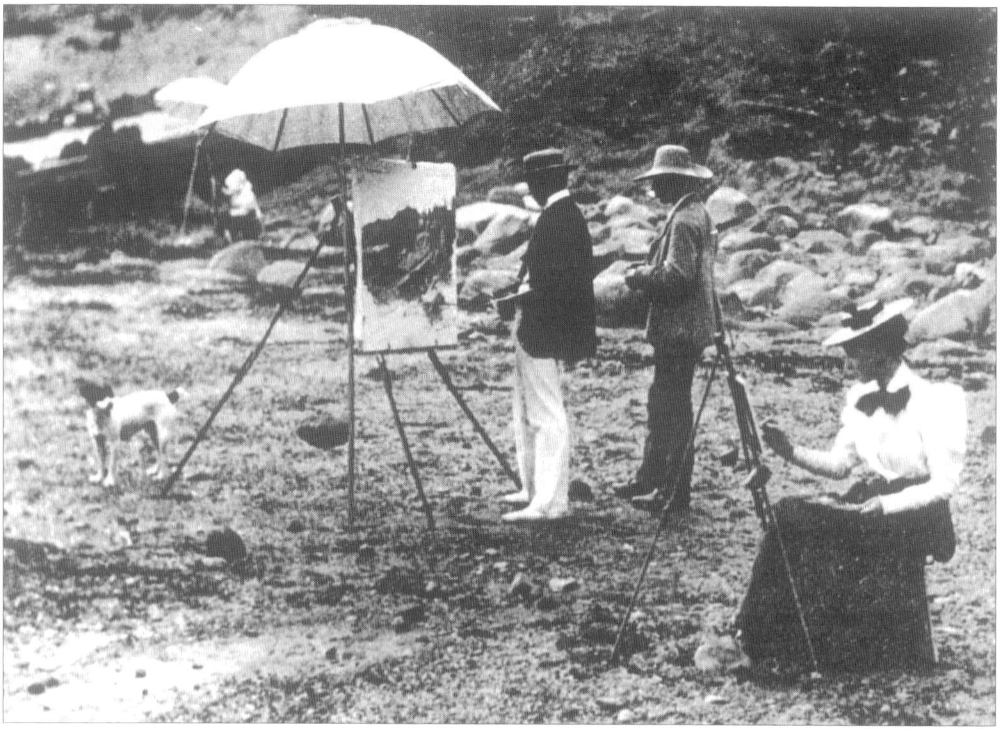

32 En Plein Air

Most of the artists at Staithes were committed to working en plein air, *outside the studio in the open air, painting directly from life. They were preoccupied, too, with light and colour. This photograph shows, standing at the easel, Fred Jackson (1859-1918), and, seated, Laura Johnson (later Dame Laura Knight) (1877-1970). The place is Runswick Bay, a tiny fishing village just round the headland from Staithes. Judging by the painters' dress and the parasols, it is summertime.*

the aristocracy and the rising middle classes enjoyed unprecedented luxury, many working people endured extreme poverty and insecurity, especially when ill health or unemployment struck. Still, for Joseph and Mildred the advent of the 20th century seemed to herald the start of a happy, loving, long life together.

Four
All Good Things ...

Although Joseph Bagshawe came from a well-to-do background – and his fiancee's family were, if anything, even more prosperous – he was now faced with the prospect of soon having to provide for a wife and, doubtless, in due course, children of his own. In other words, as a professional artist, he needed to sell his work. The same was true for almost all the artists clustered in and around Staithes. Most were of middle-class origin; a handful came from working-class backgrounds; and a very few had rich parents. The majority hailed from the West Riding of Yorkshire or Lancashire, with a scattering from Tyneside and Scotland. Rowland Hill's father was a Halifax cloth merchant; Fred Mayor, the son of a clergyman, had been educated at King's School, Canterbury; Fred Jackson's father was a photographer; Lionel Crawshaw had trained as a solicitor after taking his degree at Cambridge; and A.G. Stevens was the son of a doctor. James Booth, like his contemporary Fred Jackson, grew up in Middleton near Manchester, where his father was a rich businessman, a pillar of the local Conservative establishment, whose racehorses were trained at the same stable as those of Lord Roseberry.

From its inception in 1887 (the first exhibition was held in Bradford the following year), the Yorkshire Union of Artists attracted several of the Staithes painters, a number of whom served as Council members and office-holders;[1] but by the turn of the century a growing need was felt by the Staithes artists to have their own selling exhibitions. Consequently, it was decided at a meeting held in July 1901 that a Staithes Group of Artists should be formally constituted and that an exhibition of work by its members should be held in the upper room of the Fishermen's Institute.

Harold Hopwood was elected chairman and Thomas Barrett (who had taught Laura Johnson and Harold Knight at the Nottingham School of Art and who had advised Laura to seek out Staithes as a place to paint) was appointed treasurer. Joseph Bagshawe became secretary of the Group, an office that he held with distinction until he resigned (for reasons that will become apparent later) in 1905, and was replaced by Fred Jackson.

The first exhibition of the work of the Staithes Group of Artists appears to have been held in September 1901. Unlike future exhibitions, no detailed report of

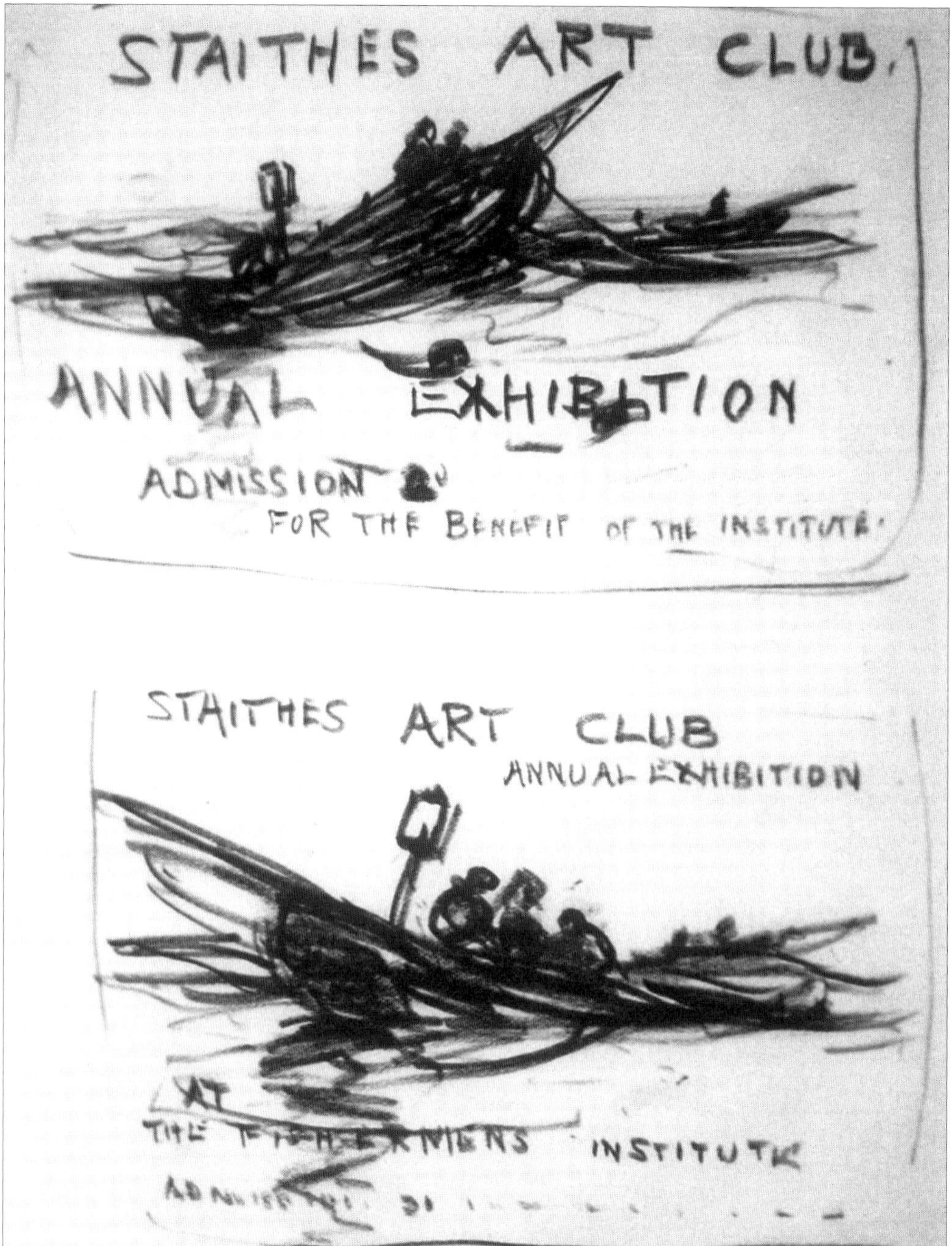

33 Staithes Art Club

In 1901, it was decided to form a Staithes Art Club (often referred to as the Staithes Group of Artists). It had no formal constitution or ideology. Harold Hopwood was elected chairman and Thomas Barret was appointed treasurer. Joseph Bagshawe was the Club's founding secretary and much of the responsibility for organising the annual exhibitions seems to have fallen on him. The first exhibition was held in the upper room of the Fishermen's Institute, Staithes, and in one of Joseph's sketchbooks drafts of possible posters have survived.

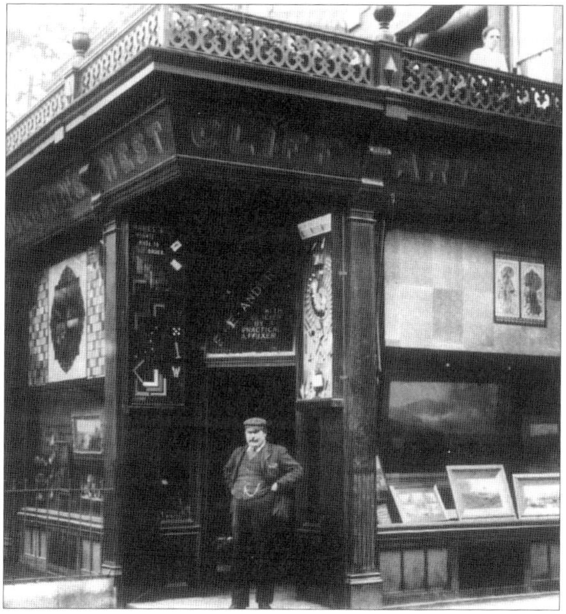

34 **Anderson's West Cliff Gallery, Skinner Street, Whitby**

In 1904, the Staithes Art Group's annual exhibition moved from Staithes, where since its foundation it had been held in the Fishermen's Institute to Whitby. There were probably two reasons for this: first, because the premises in Staithes became somewhat cramped, given the number of artists wishing to exhibit; and, second, because of the greater number of visitors to the resort and, therefore, the prospect of increased sales.

Edward Enoch Anderson, R.B.A., was a Whitby-born artist and member of the Staithes Group, whose father was a fine art dealer and proprietor of the West Cliff Gallery in Skinner Street (just a very short distance from Mulgrave Place where the Bagshawe family used to stay). Edward's studio was close by in Well Close Square, which in August 1904 was the venue for the Group's fourth annual exhibition. The Whitby Gazette *commented (18 August 1904) that: 'It seems mainly owing to Mr. J.R. Bagshawe's enterprise that the exhibition has, this year, enlarged its borders, by adding to the size and importance of the works shown; and we congratulate that energetic and able artist on the measure of success he has attained for the club's effort.'*

it was published in the *Whitby Gazette*, but a piece by a correspondent signing herself 'Kathleen' was reprinted from the *Leeds Mercury* in the Whitby paper, which stated: 'It [the exhibition] gives the general public an opportunity of seeing the quality – in many cases very high – of the pictures turned out'. Moreover:

> I have repeatedly said during the last fifteen years that I think the time is coming – if it has not already quite come – when Staithes and Runswick – especially Staithes – will be very formidable rivals as painting grounds to Newlyn and Clovelly, not alone because of their rival picturesqueness, and the archaic 'ways' of some of their people – but because they are so situated that it is next to impossible to modernise or over-build them. There is scarcely a square foot of ground to spare in either precipitous village; and in Staithes especially, the dress of the fisher-folk is as quaint and paintable as it has ever been for many generations.[2]

The reference to the West Country fishing villages serves as a reminder that by the late 19th century there were a good number of well-defined groups of artists dotted around the coasts of northern Europe.[3] They were to be found in Brittany (especially in Concarneau) and Normandy; in Holland (particularly at Scheveningen); and at Skagen on the northern tip of Denmark. A flourishing community of Scottish artists was centred on Cockburnspath in East Lothian, while a similar colony had grown up in the Northumberland fishing village of Cullercoats near the mouth of the Tyne, the place chosen by Winslow Homer in which to live and paint after he came to England in 1881. Walberswick in Suffolk also attracted artists, including the English impressionist Philip Wilson Steer (1860-1942), perhaps the only painter fully meriting that description.

As the extract from 'Kathleen''s article suggests, one of the attractions of these places was their scenic beauty, and also the quaintness of their inhabitants and their dwellings ('quaint' is an adjective that often crops up – even today – in descriptions of Whitby and its neighbouring coastal villages). But there was also the fact that these clusters of artists provided opportunities to exchange experiences, discuss techniques and to evaluate finished paintings. However, in all these colonies the commercial imperative was at work, too. The money brought in by sales was needed to pay for materials, rents, models (even though a child in Staithes would often pose for hours in return for a few coppers), and for subsistence. Above all, sales were in their way indicators of success – no painter would deny that as the prices paid for his or her paintings rose, so did the artist's feeling of self-worth.

With the inauguration of the Staithes Group of Artists and the organisation and publicising that attended its first exhibition, Joseph Bagshawe, as secretary, must have been extremely busy during the summer of 1901. So, it was all the more remarkable that he managed to cope with these duties while at the same time preparing for his marriage to Mildred, which took place at St Hilda's Roman Catholic Church, Whitby, on 3 September.

The wedding was a sumptuous affair, the like of which Whitby had never seen before – or since. The town was *en fête*. 'In honour of the event', wrote the *Whitby Gazette*, 'many parts of the town were gay with bunting, several yachts and other boats in the harbour being hung with flags, as was also a new vessel recently launched from the [bride's father's] Whitehall Shipyard. The National Ensign floated from the tower of St Mary's [Anglican] Parish Church, and the bells rang out a merry peal during the day.'[4]

In order to avoid a crush, admission to the church was by printed invitation only. The congregation came from far and wide. The entire elite of Whitby seemed to be there, as well as a strong contingent from Ardrossan in Scotland (Mildred's mother's family and friends) and another from Antwerp, which may have had a shipping connection with the Turnbulls. Naturally, there were many Bagshawes, too; and a good few august titles peppered the long list of invited guests.

> When Mildred entered the church on her father's arm: She looked extremely pretty in a dress of tucked *crepe de Chine* over white silk, Court train from the shoulders of white Duchesse satin, embroidered with true lover's knots in chiffon and orange blossom, lined with white rucked chiffon; the bodice being composed of finely tucked *crepe de Chine* trimmed with Limerick lace (the gift of her mother); and a tulle veil fastened with diamond stars over a coronet of orange blossom. She also wore ornaments of pearls and diamonds, the gifts of her parents; and carried a bouquet of stephanotis, white heather, and roses, the gift of the bridegroom.

Similar sartorial details were recounted in the *Whitby Gazette*'s descriptions of Mildred's train bearers, her bridesmaids, and of Mrs Turnbull, the mother of the bride, who 'was attired in a lovely dress of painted *mousselcine de soie*, with *applique* of black lace insertion over pale-blue silk', and concluded, 'many of the lady guests wore magnificent costumes'.

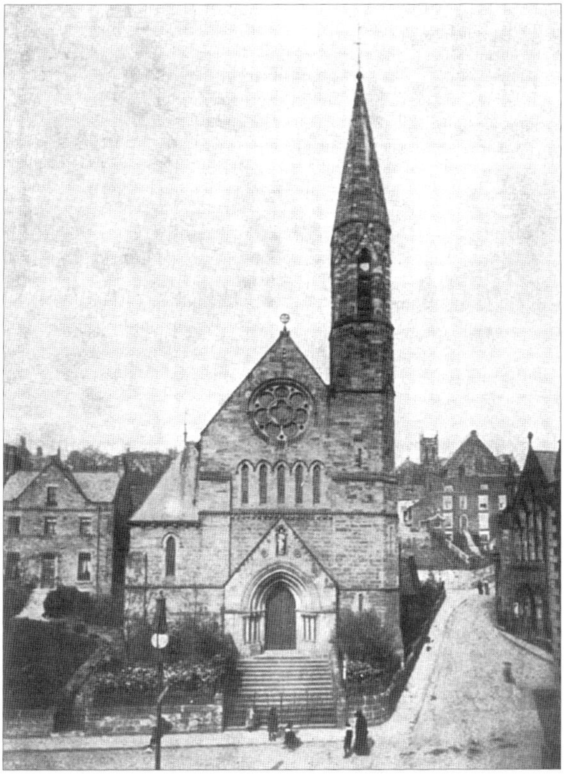

35 Marriage
Having kept their engagement from public view from September 1898 to Valentine's Day 1901, in September that year Joseph and Mildred were married in St Hilda's Roman Catholic Church, Whitby. The church stands at the foot of Brunswick Street. At the side opposite is St John's Church (Church of England) and higher up the hill is Brunswick Methodist Church – little wonder that locals referred to it as 'Amen Corner'. The wedding was a sumptuous affair and the Whitby Gazette *carried a detailed report of it, mentioning by name not only the guests, but also the presents they had given the bride and groom.*

The service was conducted by the Right Reverend the Archbishop of Heliopolis, Dr Bagshawe, the uncle of the bridegroom, assisted by several local clergy. Far from all the guests were Catholics: the congregation included 'a large proportion to whom the service was strange'. Mildred's brother, Tertius, at the commencement of the Nuptial Mass sang the Pater Noster 'in Niedermeyer's beautiful setting ... in a most reverent and effective manner'. Finally, following the Episcopal blessing, the wedding party left the church, to be greeted with showers of confetti, before making their way by carriage to Airy Hill, where 'Dyson's band, from Leeds, discoursed some favourite selections in the garden during the reception', after which the bridal couple caught the afternoon train from nearby Ruswarp as they set off for their honeymoon in Ireland. It had, indeed, been a day that 'for brilliance, has seldom, if ever, been rivalled in Whitby'.

But it is not just the sumptuousness of the wedding itself that strikes the reader; there was yet more to come. The *Gazette*'s listing of the guests was followed by a catalogue of the presents ('unusually handsome and costly') that Joseph and Mildred had received – the details of which must have been supplied by the Turnbulls – and which today seem to be almost embarrassingly ostentatious; yet that was the custom at the time and so not particularly unusual.

The bridegroom had given the bride a diamond ring, topaz necklace, a spade guinea, a bracelet, otter skin rug and a silver casket. The bride's father gave a diamond and pearl brooch, a pearl necklet, a cheque, dressing bag, and fish knives and forks; while the bride's mother gave furs, a pearl brooch, a bureau, household linen, silver cake basket, silver candlesticks, lace and furniture. Amongst the presents given by Tertius, Mildred's brother, was a Bechstein piano. On Joseph's side, Judge and Mrs Bagshawe's presents included a cheque, Sheraton sideboard, chairs, entrée dishes, a travelling clock, and a picture by the late Clarkson Stanfield, R.A.

With the immediate families out of the way, there followed column inch after column inch listing the other guests and itemising the presents they had given. There was a veritable cascade of silver and choice porcelain: tea services, cutlery, photograph frames, fruit dishes, fish carvers, soup tureen, to mention but a few. The office staff at the Whitehall Shipyard gave a set of silver and ivory dessert knives and forks; while the manager, foreman and workmen at the yard had clubbed together to buy the couple a silver coffee pot and cake basket: not to be outdone, the servants at Airy Hill (much smaller in number) gave a silver salver (Harold Smales, evidently still unmarried, also chose to give a silver salver). The clergy were fairly predictable. Father McCabe's present was a silver crucifix in a case; Father Ryan presented the newlyweds with a shillelagh and bog oak bellows; the Rev. Donald Skrimshire gave a New Testament; and the Bishop of Nottingham (another of Joseph's uncles) presented the couple with a set of Papal coins.

Amongst the guests were listed several artists: Mr Knight gave a picture; so did Miss L. Johnson. T.C. Alder, an amateur artist who worked as a draughtsman for Thomas Turnbull & Sons (and whose wife, as it happens, was organist at St Hilda's Roman Catholic Church), also gave a painting; as did Mr S. Richardson. Mr and Mrs Hopwood's present was a copy of Ruskin's *Architecture and Painting*. Then, towards the end of the list, appears a Miss Ellen Verrill, who gave a modest tray cloth.

A search of the 1901 Census reveals that Ellen Verrill was the 23-year-old eldest child of Ann Verrill, who kept a grocery shop at 36 High Street, Staithes. Until this information came to light it had been a puzzle as to where Joseph lodged when he was painting at Staithes. Now it seems very likely that Ann Verrill was his landlady, although it was red-haired Ellen who was invited to attend the wedding. One suspects (or, rather, one hopes) that her tray cloth was treasured just as much as the other 'unusually handsome and costly' wedding presents on display that day.

In contrast, however, there was one unusually handsome and extremely generous present *not* on display. It was a yacht. Given by Thomas Turnbull to his new son-in-law personally, it was intended not so much for recreational and sporting use, but, rather, as we shall see presently, in order to facilitate Joseph's career as a marine painter.

All good things, as they say, must come to an end. And so it was with 1901, that memorable year when Joseph and Mildred had formally become engaged and then married in such splendour. A little under two months after the wedding, on 30 October 1901, one of Joseph's uncles, John Bernard Bagshawe, a Roman Catholic priest, died at the age of 73 from complications following influenza. Then, just five days later, his brother (Joseph's father, W.H.G. Bagshawe) died from cardiac failure: he collapsed on the platform at King's Cross Station, and was buried in St Mary's Cemetery, Kensal Green, following a Requiem Mass conducted by another brother, Canon Bagshawe, Archbishop of Heliopolis, who only the month before had married Joseph and Mildred in Whitby.

36 *As well as craft from East Anglia and Scotland, each year Whitby was visited in August and September by luggers from Cornwall, the 'Penzancemen', so-called because their port of registration was Penzance (PZ). The postcard below was produced by the well-known local photographer, J.T. Ross, a former shipwright in Mildred's father's Whitehall yard.*

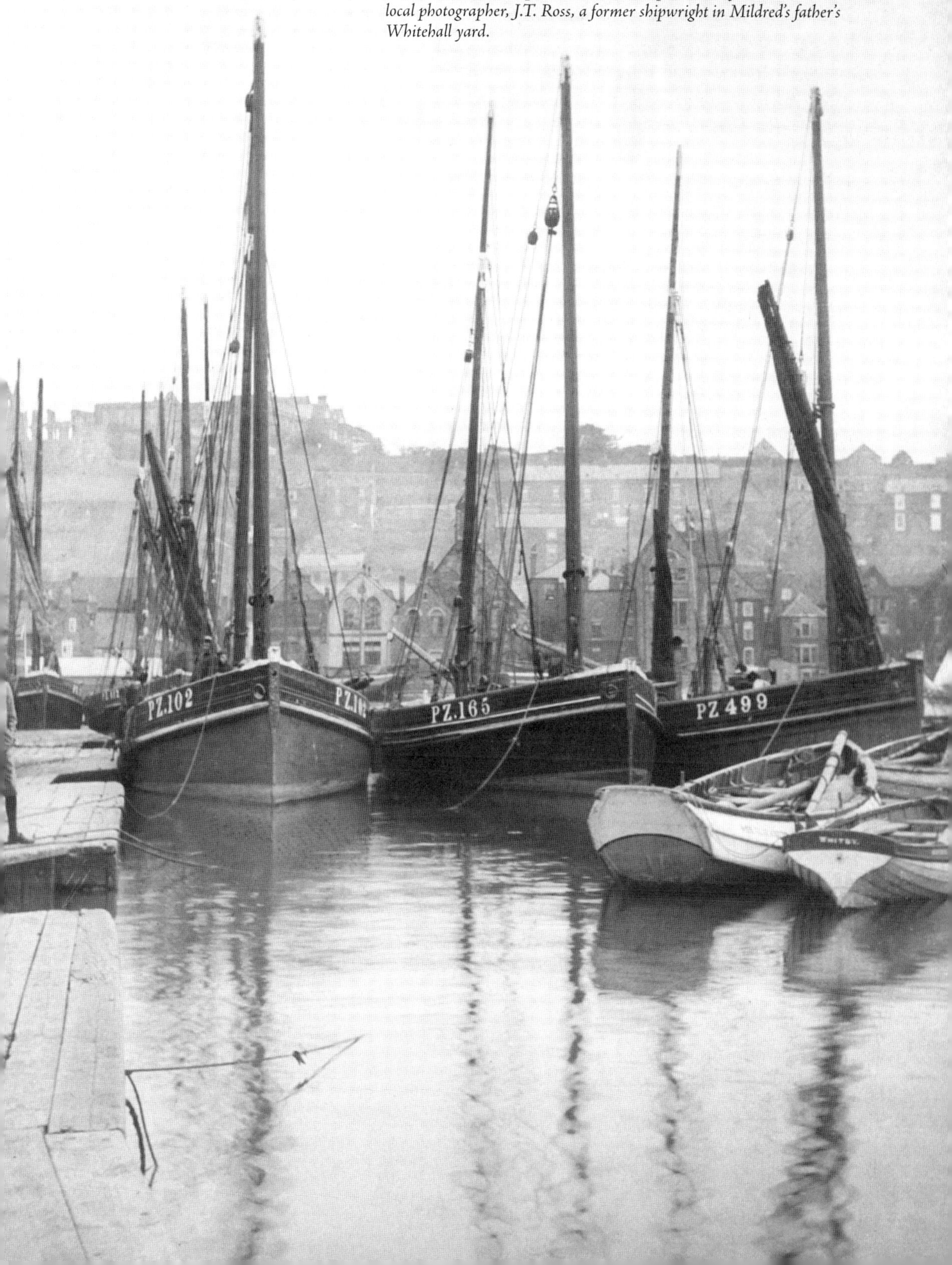

These events, in quick succession, came as a double blow to Joseph, particularly since he was with his father when he died: he fell, wrote Mildred later, 'into my dear Joe's arms in King's Cross Station. This was the beginning of all our trouble, for the shock so affected his digestion that he never got it right again.' In fact, the problem was not Joe's digestion; it was sugar diabetes, although it was 1906, nearly five years later, before this was correctly diagnosed. He had been visiting Ardrossan in Scotland, where his wife's mother's family lived, when he fell ill. 'A few days after his return to Whitby the doctor discovered that he had diabetes, very badly; in fact, he gave him only three weeks to live.'

Rather than three weeks, Joseph lived for another three years. So it was that for their entire married life together he and Mildred were plagued by Joe's ill health. The severity of the disease ebbed and flowed, but it was ever present. Cures were attempted (the discovery of insulin by the Canadian medical scientists Dr Frederick Banting and Dr Charles Best of the University of Toronto, for which they were awarded Nobel prizes in 1923, was still 14 years away) and there were periods of remission, but, in the end, they were to no avail and Joseph died, cradled in his wife's arms, on 1 November 1909 at their home in Whitby.

Throughout these years, Joseph and Mildred lived their lives together with great intensity. They never gave up hope. Mildred bore three sons; they were a blessedly happy family. They socialised and travelled and were inconspicuously active in public life. Nor did Joseph give up on his painting; far from it. In fact, he was entering upon the most fruitful phase of his career as an artist. Success followed upon success and there is little doubt but that eventually he would have achieved widespread national acclaim and almost certainly membership of the Royal Academy. After all, he was just 39 when he died and approaching the peak of his powers. However, this is to run ahead of the story.

Joseph and Mildred stayed on in London for two months following Judge Bagshawe's death, while Joseph dealt with his father's affairs; after which they returned to Whitby and rented Moss Brow, a stone-built

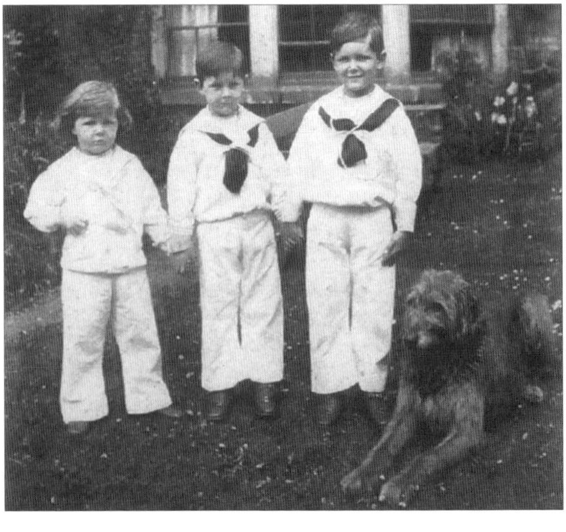

37 Sailor Suits

This photograph was taken on the lawn in front of the Old Rectory, Bagdale, Whitby, in 1908 by J.T. Ross. It shows Joseph and Mildred's three sons (from left to right) Wilfrid, George and Edward (aged respectively three, five and six). The family pet (an Irish wolfhound) was called Colin. It was Joseph's hope that his sons might grow up to become officers in the Royal Navy (none did), but the sailor suits they are wearing in this photograph were probably simply a reflection of the current fashion for boys (and girls) in the Edwardian period.

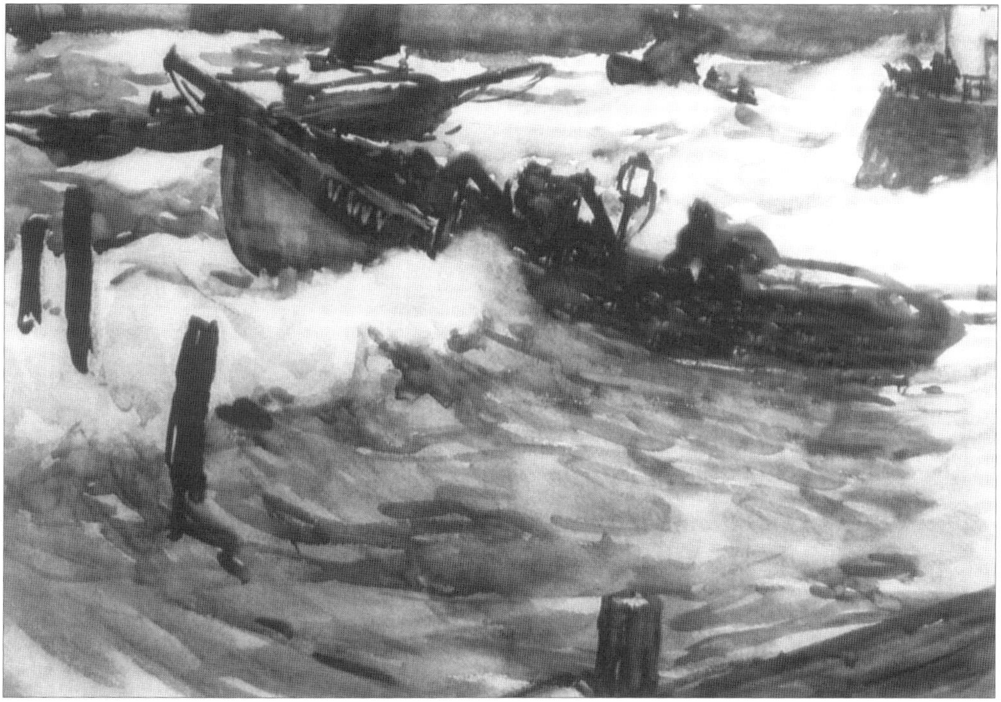

38 *Cobles Setting off from Staithes in a Stormy Sea*
This watercolour is characteristic of the free-flowing, broad-brush, impressionistic style that Joseph favoured increasingly in his later years. The paintings that he submitted for exhibition at the Royal Academy each summer were executed in oils, but it was his watercolours that often better captured the movement of the sea.

property, owned by the Pymans, a shipping family, situated on a prominent elevation halfway between Whitby and Sandsend. To the east stands Whitby Abbey, facing the German Ocean (as the North Sea was known at that time), and to the west Sandsend Ness; while, looking out to sea, shipping was constantly in sight, passing up and down the coast between the coal ports of Durham and Northumberland to the north and London, with its voracious appetite for fuel to the south. We were 'perfectly happy and cosy' there, recalled Mildred, and it was at Moss Brow that the first of their three sons, George, was born in September 1904. It was round about this time, too, that Joseph visited St Ives, Penzance and Falmouth, staying longest, about two or three weeks, at St Ives. These places were, of course, where groups of artists had congregated, although they do not appear to have tempted Joseph away from the wild Yorkshire coast. He must, however, have found it interesting to see at first hand the home ports of the 'Penzancemen', the boats that each late summer crowded Whitby harbour, together with Scottish boats and craft from East Anglia, all gathered there for the herring fishery, and with whose crews Joseph was to become so familiar.

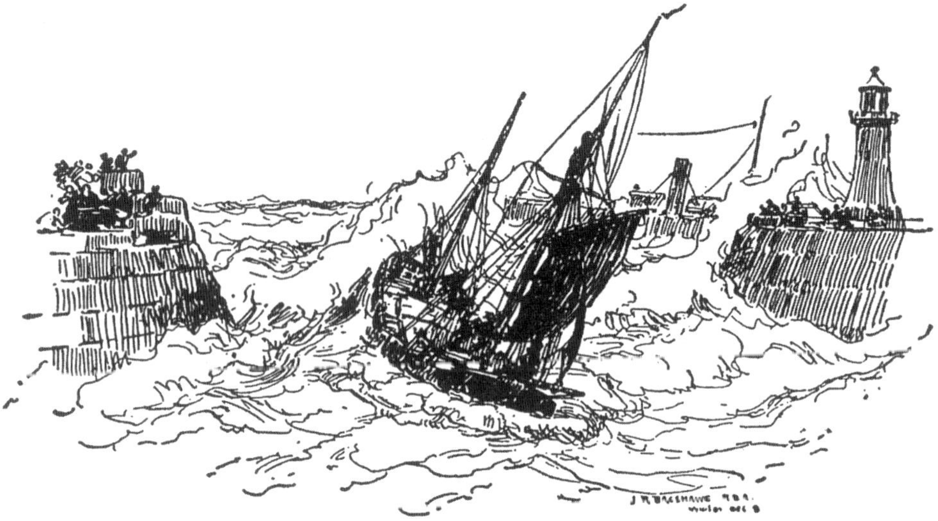

39 *In the last two years of his life, Joseph branched out in a literary direction. As well as his paintings, he began to write articles for various periodicals, doubtless in order to increase his income, but also to demonstrate a literary talent (his factual articles were much, much better than his earlier attempts at fiction). His prose was enhanced by illustrative line drawings, which demonstrate that he was quite capable of precise representations, as well as his impressionistic use of paint.*

The drawing above appeared in The Daily Graphic *of 11 December 1906. It shows a tragic incident that occurred when the barge* Star of Colchester *attempted to cross the treacherous harbour bar, seeking refuge in a storm. In 'full view of the hundreds of persons on the piers, the coastguard, and the rocket battery', the mate was swept off the deck and drowned. The tragedy finally persuaded the Board of Trade that improvements to the harbour entrance were needed urgently and as a result pier extensions were built. Between the barge and the East Pier lighthouse, a steamer can be seen in the background: she was the Isle of Iona that had foundered on the rocks at the approach to the harbour.*

It was in 1904, too, that Joseph earned the right to place the letters RBA (Fellow of the Royal Society of British Artists) after his name, a practice that he almost always adhered to from then on. Four of his paintings, including *Herring Fishers* and *Off to the Fishing Ground*, were hung at the RBA that year, as was *A Summer's Day off Whitby* at the Royal Academy's summer show, all indications of his growing stature as an artist.

Despite the anxiety and distraction occasioned by his illness, Joseph now threw himself into his work with ever greater vigour and, in fact, the period from 1904 until his death in November 1909 was the most productive of his entire career. It was at about this time that he further developed his fluent, free-flowing style of painting, extended the geographical range of his choice of subject, and, not least, showed himself to be no mean writer of prose, work that, while staying with the sea and those who sailed upon it as its themes, was illustrated with attractive, skilful, technically accurate line drawings. In short, all this, taken together, constituted a new chapter in the artistic career of Joseph Bagshawe, RBA.

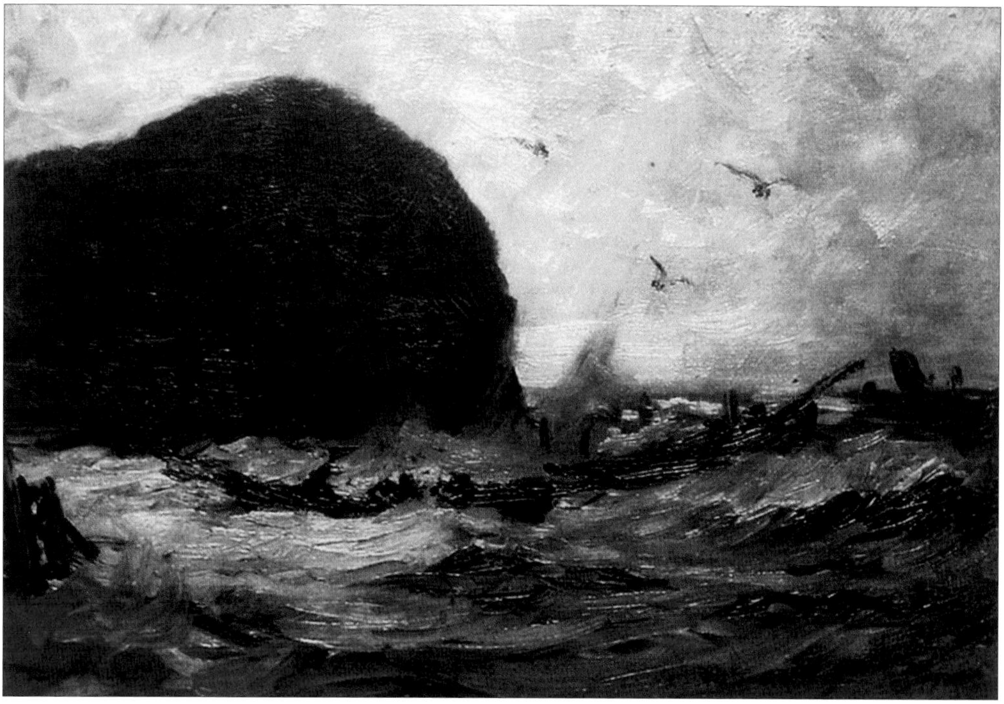

I Sea Painter

Like his grandfather before him, Joseph Bagshawe was a consummate painter of the sea, whether it was storm or calm, rough or still. Both of the pictures shown on this page are painted from the same viewpoint; both show the huge bulk of Cowbar Nab, Staithes, in the background, and both depict cobles putting to sea for a night's fishing. In the first painting, however, Bagshawe captures the turbulence of waves rushing towards the shore, with a stormy sky above and the boats cresting the breakers. The second painting (oil on canvas, 24 x 36ins, signed, exhibited at the Royal Academy in 1904 under the title A Nor'wester*), below, is of an oily swell, with the only white water being a low fringe at the base of the Nab as the rollers meet the shore. A north-westerly at Staithes is an offshore wind.*

2

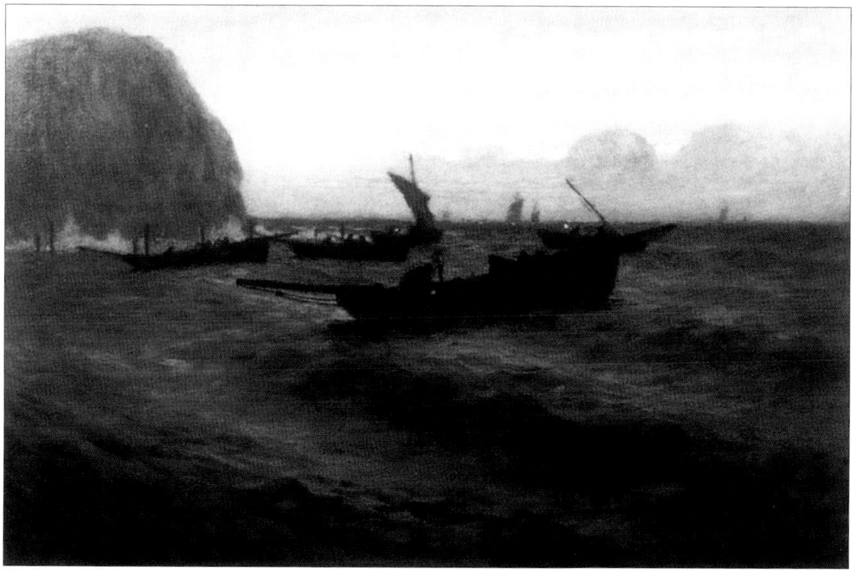

3

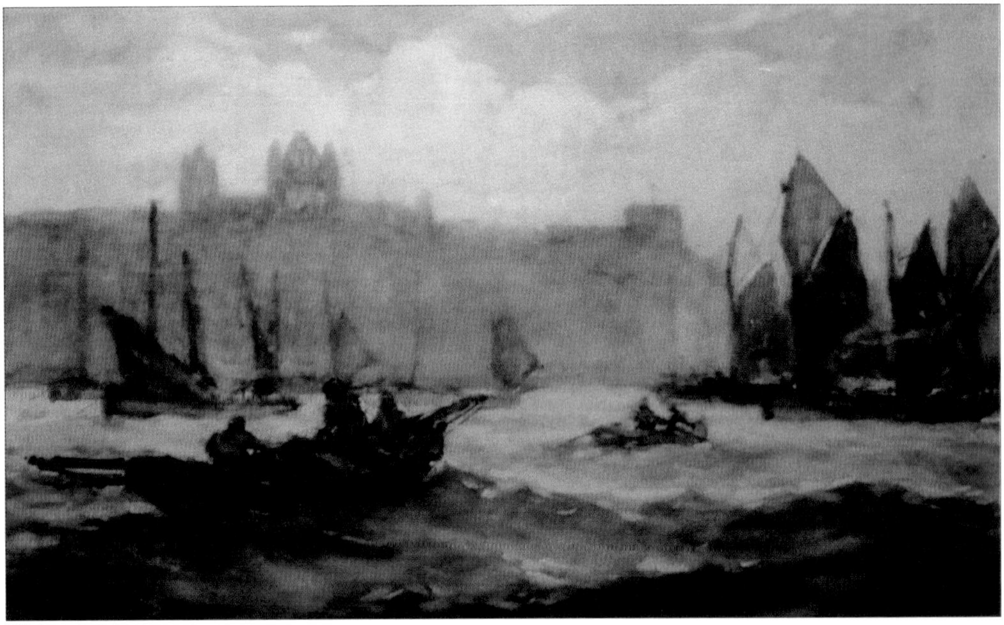

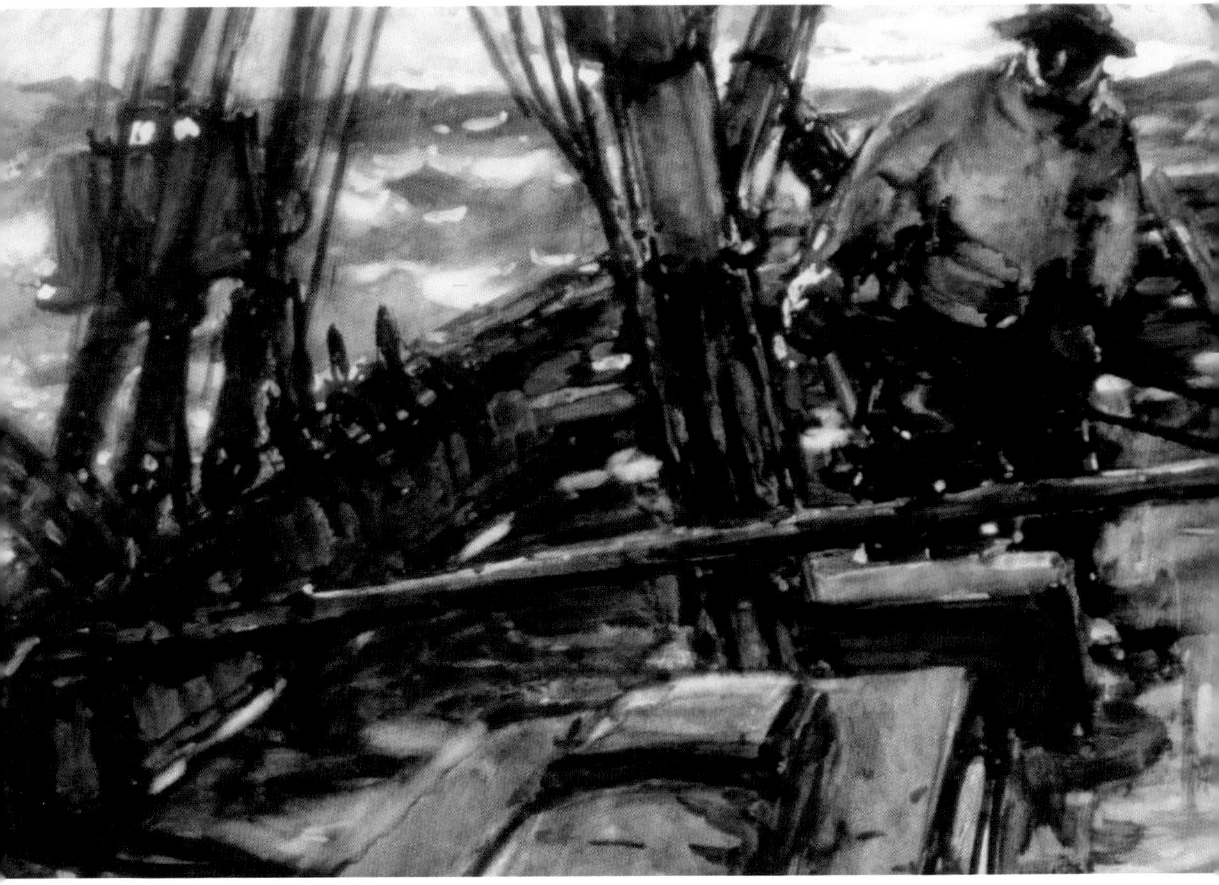

4

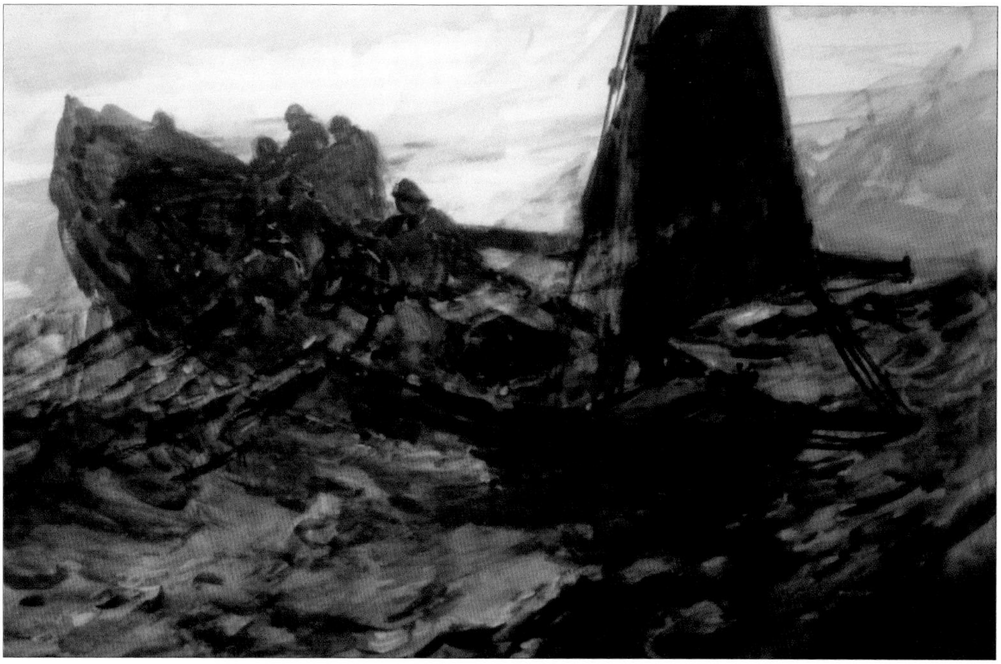

3 *(Facing page, top) Following the death of Joseph's father towards the end of 1901, just a few months after their marriage, Joseph and Mildred remained in London clearing up the late judge's affairs. They then returned to Whitby, where they rented a house, Moss Brow, belonging to the Pymans, a ship-owning family, where the first of their three sons was born in September 1904. The house looked out over the sea, with Sandsend Ness to the West and Whitby Abbey and the parish church on the headland to the east.*

Joseph's watercolour of Whitby from the sea shows the Abbey and St Mary's parish church atop the East Cliff, with a variety of fishing craft congregating off the harbour mouth. On the right, are tall, stately luggers from East Anglia ('Lowstermen'), while on the left are Scottish boats, all at Whitby for the herring season. In the foreground is a Yorkshire, three-man coble, riding the 'jowly' (choppy) sea, which, as always with Bagshawe, is evoked in a masterly way.

4 'Owd John'

(Opposite) The skipper of the True Love *was John Thompson, known as 'Owd John' to distinguish him from his son John, who was one of the crew of the yawl. While at sea, Joseph made numerous sketches of the boat, her crew and the fishing, many of which as line drawings appear as illustrations to his article 'A Week in a Long-Liner'. Back on shore, he painted at least one picture of his trip. It is entitled* The Old Skipper in a Squall *and hangs in the Pannett Art Gallery at Whitby Museum. Typically for Joseph, it has been painted quickly with free-flowing brush strokes, and the motion of the yawl on a turbulent sea is captured brilliantly, not least by having 'Owd John' lean to his left, while the boat itself, forced by the wind and waves, inclines to his right, thus setting up a tension between the mast and rigging and the skipper. Also, the splash of light shining through the hatch in the centre foreground suggests that while the rest of the crew are snug below, the old man on deck is engaged in his struggle with the elements.*

5 *(Above) This picture is typical of the kind of scene that Joseph might have witnessed when he went off in his yacht* Beatrice. *It shows the crew of a large herring coble (a plosher) hauling in their nets against a breaking dawn sky. Joseph was sometimes criticised on the grounds that his paintings were too dark and sombre. What those critics forgot was that a great deal of fishing activity takes place at night, or at dawn and dusk. There is no minute detail in this picture, no precise delineation; yet overall it is absolutely authentic in the way that the coble is poised at precisely the correct angle to the waves, which in turn are captured in motion by the fluid use of paint.*

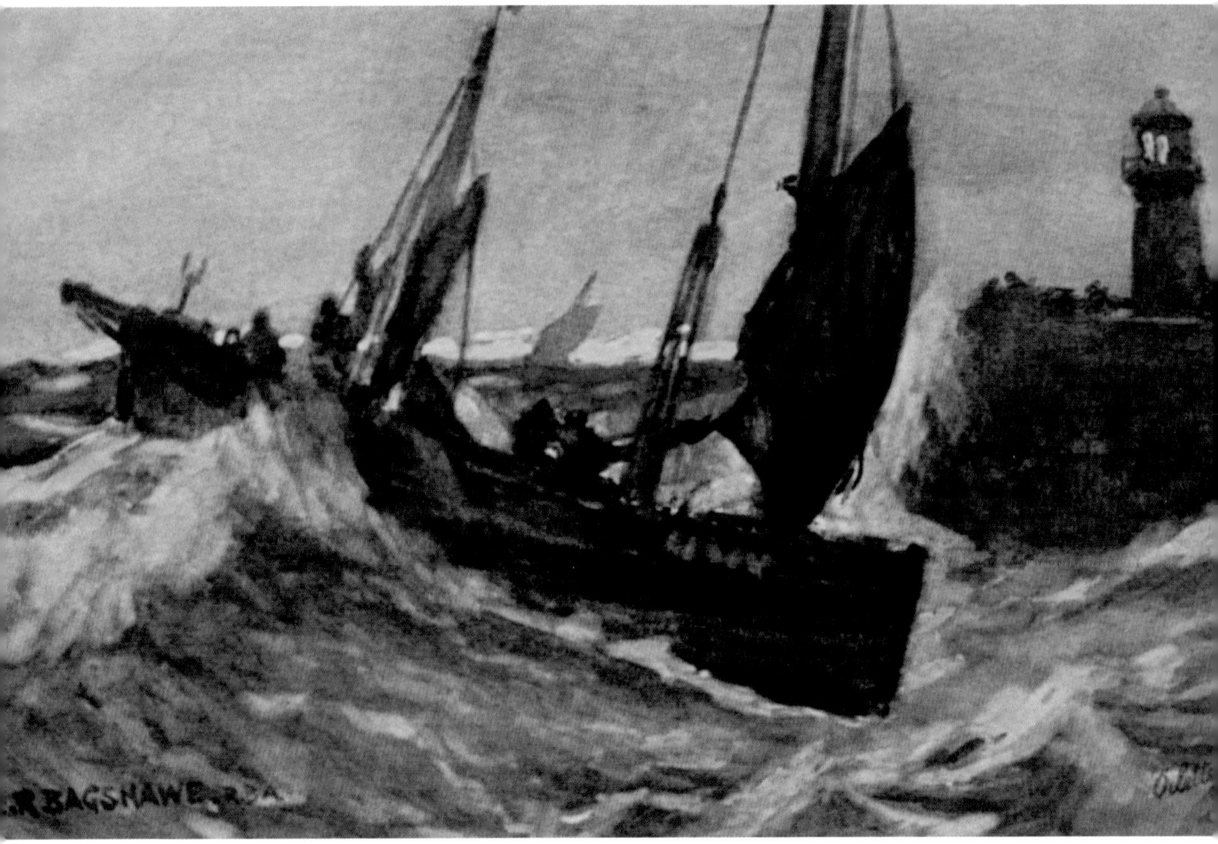

6 Over the Bar

This is one of a series of Bagshawe's paintings reproduced on postcards by Raphael Tuck and Sons around about 1908. It shows a Scottish herring boat crossing the treacherous bar at the entrance to Whitby harbour, with the East Pier lighthouse on the right. One can sense the surge of the waves as the craft is thrust forward into the harbour. Dawn is just lightening in the east.

7 'A Good Haul'

(Facing page, top) This is one of the first series of six postcards published in 1907 by Raphael Tuck & Sons under the general heading Toilers of the Sea. *An undated letter to Joseph has survived from a friend named 'Cuth' which says: 'I made an honest penny the other day by doing some picture postcards for Raphael Tuck and Sons for two guineas each. I don't know whether any have been printed yet or not as I've not seen any about.' Two guineas may not seem a great amount, but it should be remembered that it is more than a week's wages for an agricultural worker at that time, so, with a growing family to support, Joseph was probably glad of any commission he could get.*

8 *(Facing page, middle) Joseph was exceptionally active in the last two years of his life, 1908 and 1909. Between bouts of ill health he made several painting forays – Normandy, Holland, Ireland. In the summer of 1908, together with his brother, Edward, who was on leave from the army, he sailed on a timber ship belonging to one of his wife's mother's family to the Baltic, visiting several ports, which, in those days, were still part of the Russian Empire. He describes the voyage in an illustrated article published in* The Yachting and Boating Monthly *of June 1908. The vessel was called the* Drumloist, *although in the article it was given the name* Drumbeath. *Joseph lived at a time when sail was still prevalent and steam did not have the overwhelming dominance that it was soon to achieve. This is a rare (perhaps unique) example of Joseph's choosing a steamer as the main subject of one of his paintings.*

7

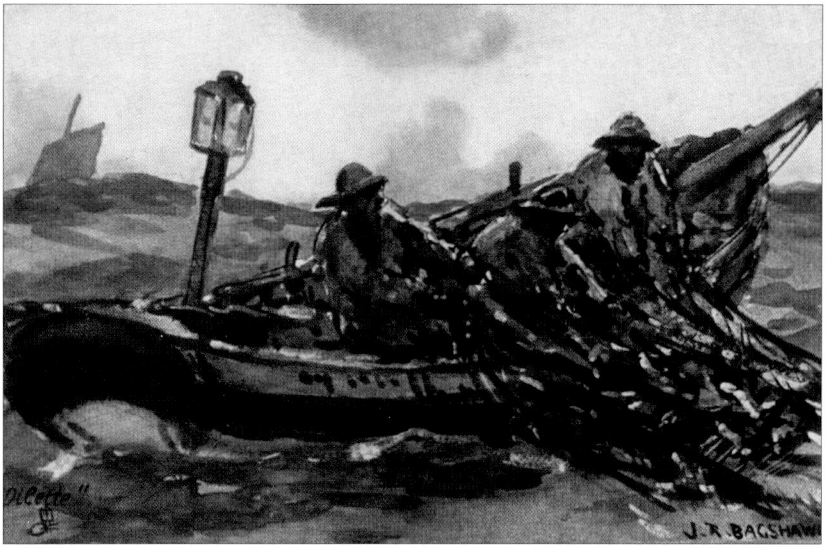

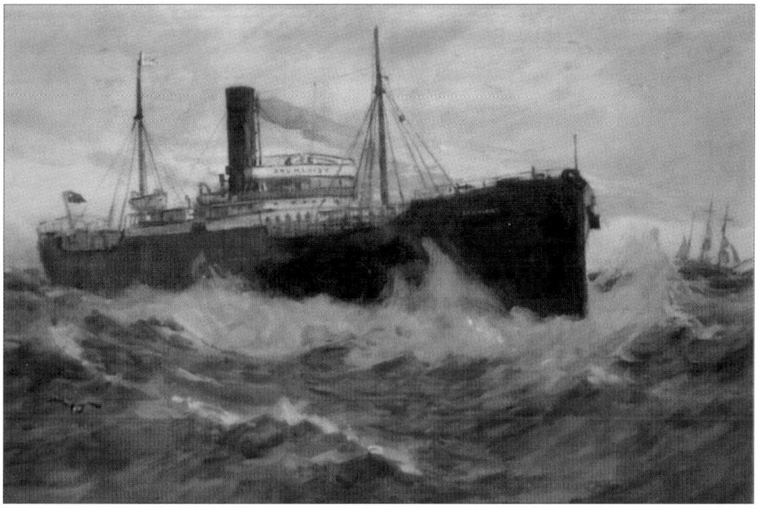

8

9 *Dutch Fishing Boats, by* J.R. Bagshawe

In 1908, the year before he died, Joseph Bagshawe went on a painting visit to the Low Countries. He was particularly interested in the fishing craft of Berck on the French Channel coast and also those of the Dutch North Sea coast, such as at Katwyk. This picture depicts a tranquil scene, yet, as always, Bagshawe's detail is authentic; while artistically the verticality of the masts bisecting the horizon draws the eye to the diagonal arrangement of the boats at anchor, with the main feature in the left foreground.

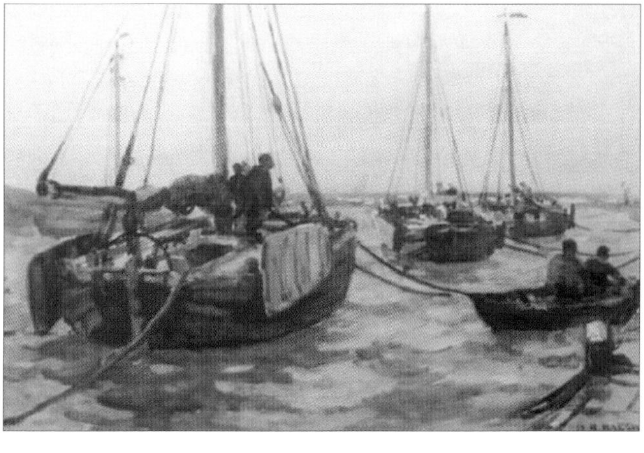

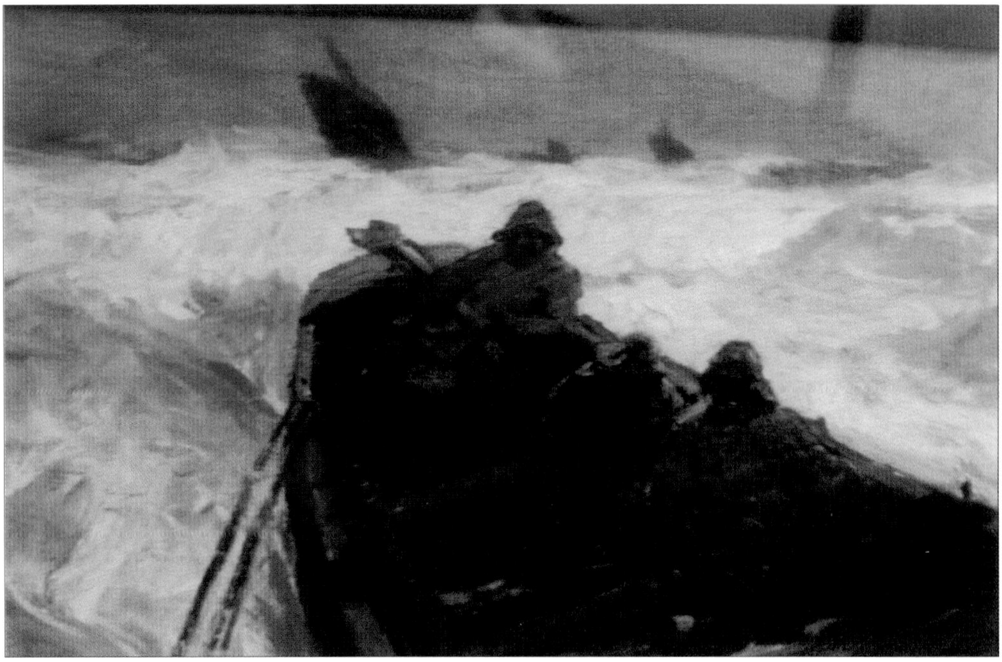

10 & 11 Moving Pictures

The early years of the 20th century saw the beginnings of film and the cinema. It was often commented that one of the principal qualities of many of Joseph's paintings was that they conveyed a strong sense of movement. It is just possible that Joseph had been influenced by the 'movies', and not least by the camera angles that were a feature of moving film, as these two paintings suggest. Untitled [white water].

11 *In the Teeth of the Gale*

From the Toilers of the Sea *series.*

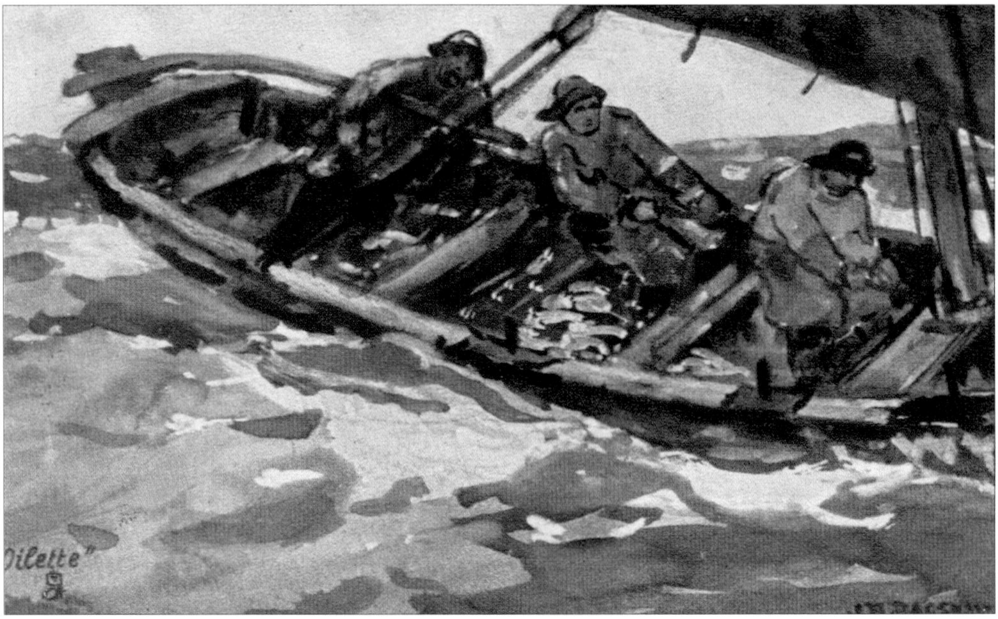

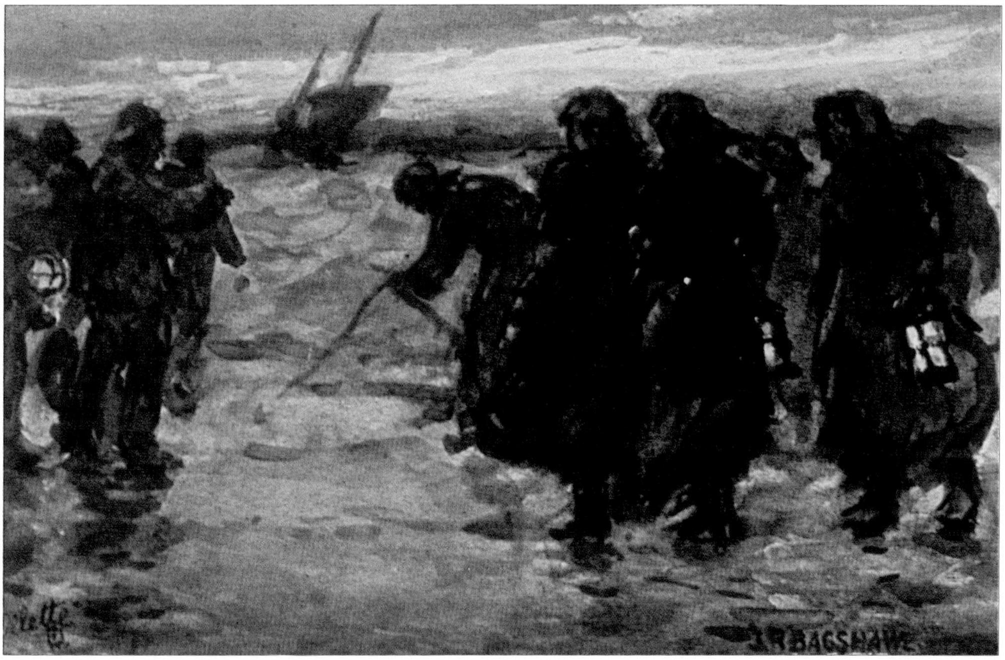

12 *In the Dawn*, from the *Toilers of the Sea* series, by Joseph Bagshawe

The setting for this scene is Staithes. It is dawn and the cobles are returning from the fishing. Down at the very edge of the sea other fishermen and several women are waiting to see the incoming crew safely ashore. Joseph Bagshawe was sometimes criticised on the grounds, it was said, that his paintings were too sombre, too dark and gloomy. Yet in fact that darkness demonstrated the realism with which he imbued his paintings. Much of the fishermen's work took place at dusk or dawn, having fished through the night. As so often in his watercolour paintings, In the Dawn *is done in an impressionistic manner, with fluid, loose brushstrokes. It is a high horizon, but already dawn is showing in the east, although the lanterns provide splashes of brightness against the dark background.*

13 *St. Valery Mackerel Boat*, from the *Toilers of the Sea* series, by Joseph Bagshawe

In an article published in The Field *in September 1909 entitled 'Some Fishing Boats of the Low Countries', Joseph described not only what might be termed the 'archaeology' of this type of boat, but also the mode of fishing for mackerel that such boats engaged in. It is obvious that he had an expert, detailed knowledge of these matters, yet, although the scene depicted here is absolutely faithful to reality, it is above all an artistic composition that typically suggests the movement of the sea and, with deft dabs of white paint, shows the mackerel being hauled aboard by the crew.*

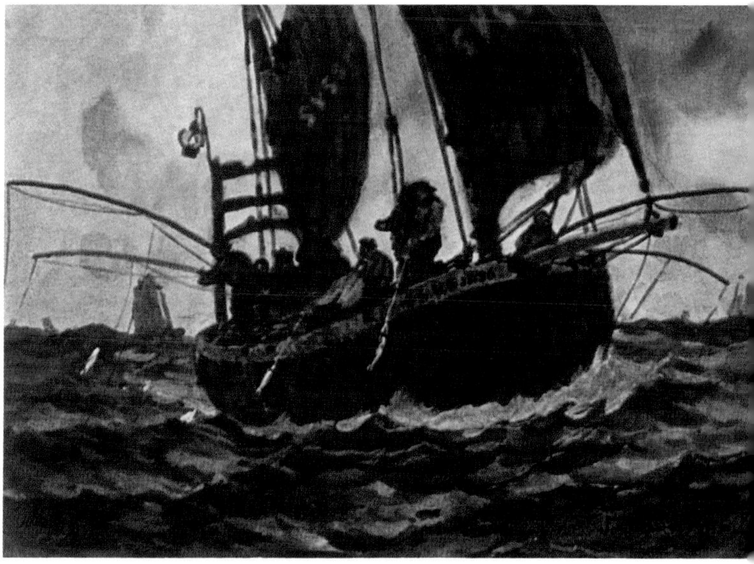

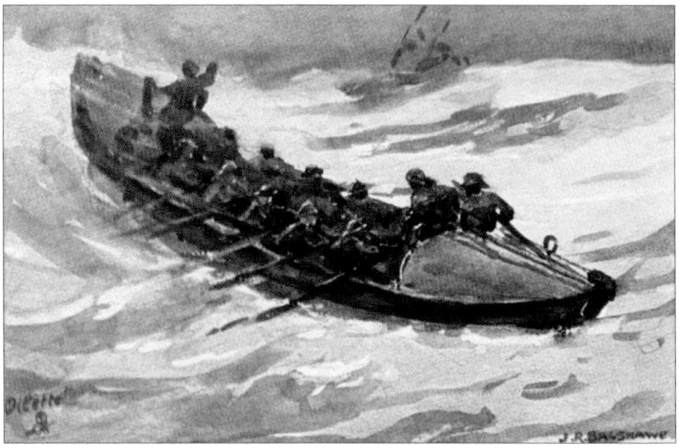

14 To The Rescue, from the Toilers of the Sea series, by J.R. Bagshawe

The original sketch for this painting may have been drawn from life. The perspective is looking down on the lifeboat with the foundering ship visible in the background. This is exactly how the scene would have appeared from the end of Whitby's West Pier just as the lifeboat was crossing the harbour bar. There is a preponderance of white in the painting, the rest being shades of black. J.M.W. Turner was extremely upset by the ridicule that one critic heaped on his painting Snow Storm – Steam Boat off a Harbour's Mouth. *It looked, said the critic, as if it had been painted in 'soapsuds and whitewash'. On reading this, Turner, who was staying at Ruskin's house, exclaimed angrily: 'Soapsuds and whitewash! I wonder what they think the sea is like? I wish they'd been in it' (Turner had himself experienced such a storm at first hand).*

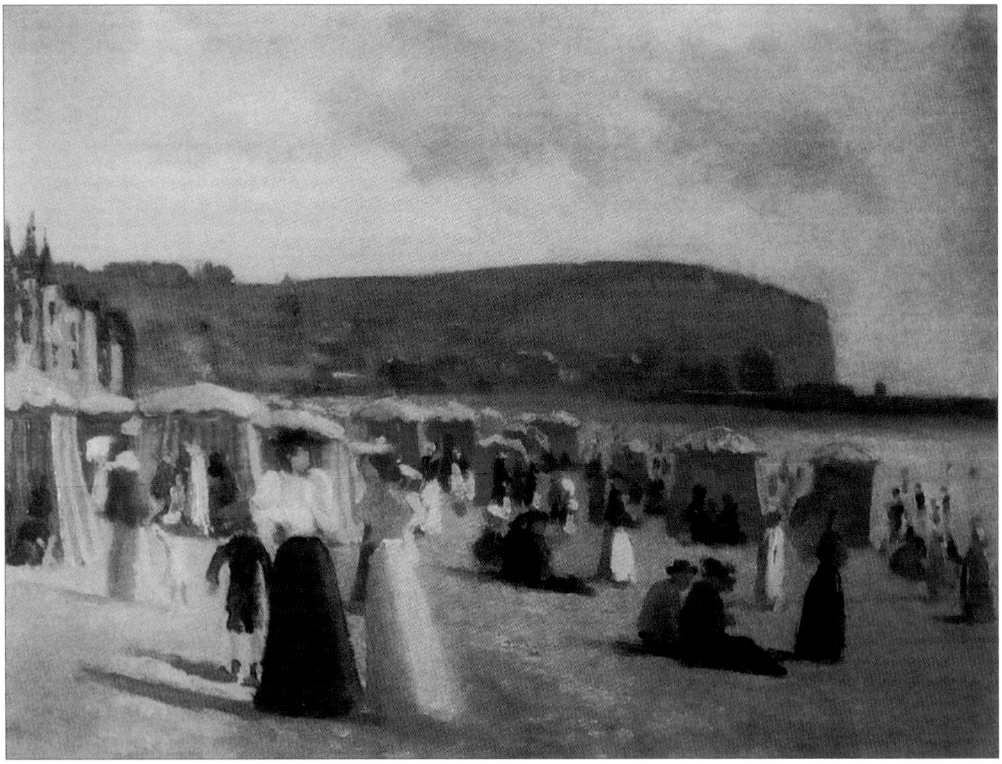

15 *The news that Joseph was suffering from sugar diabetes, for which, at that time, there was no cure, thrust the possibility of imminent death on his and Mildred's minds. Perhaps it was that which prompted them to take a holiday together in the spring of 1908. After a few days in London, they went to Margate to stay with one of Joseph's sisters, and enjoyed cycling 'all over Thanet'; it was, wrote Mildred later, 'another honeymoon'. It is quite likely that it was while they were on the Kent coast that Joseph painted this, for him, uncharacteristically colourful picture, reminiscent of the work of many Impressionist painters on the other side of the Channel.*

Five
'Baggie'

His youngest son, Wilfrid, wrote in 1933, some 24 years after Joseph Bagshawe's death, that 'my father's greatest interest was the sea.' 'All his best work had the sea in its changing moods as a setting. But from boyhood he had been a practical seaman, and he studied the sea from the fishing craft themselves, and later from his own small yacht, going out for a fortnight or more at a time, and returning with sketches that were strong and vigorous, and at the same time technically correct in practical detail.'[1]

That brief characterisation encapsulates succinctly the essence of much of Joseph's art. At the same time, it raises certain questions to which it is extremely difficult to find answers. For example, when, where and from whom in his boyhood did he learn 'practical' seamanship? His early years were spent in landlocked Hampstead, so the most likely opportunity to have presented itself may have been when he attended St Augustine's College in Ramsgate. There he looked out over the sea and onto the busy harbour every day; yet there was nothing in the school's curriculum or in recollections of his years on the Kent coast to show that he actually learned to sail there.

Beaumont College was also a good distance from the sea, although it is true that the curriculum made provision for the boys to choose 'boating' as a sporting activity. The Thames was close at hand at Windsor and small-boat sailing certainly took place at nearby Richmond, but that hardly constitutes *sea*manship. Therefore, precisely how Joseph acquired his nautical skills must remain a mystery. However, a good deal more is known about his going to sea with the fishermen themselves, and also about his yachting activities.

In the early years of the 20th century, Whitby harbour was packed every late summer with boats from all corners of the British Isles. They had gathered for the annual herring fishery that began each year in the far north of Scotland, before sailing south, arriving in mid-August and departing in September, in pursuit of the vast shoals of herring. From Whitby the fleet drifted south to Scarborough and Bridlington, and, eventually, to Yarmouth and Lowestoft, where the great migration culminated. There were boats from Ireland and the Isle of man; from the west and east coasts of Scotland; Yorkshire boats – big herring cobles (*ploshers*)

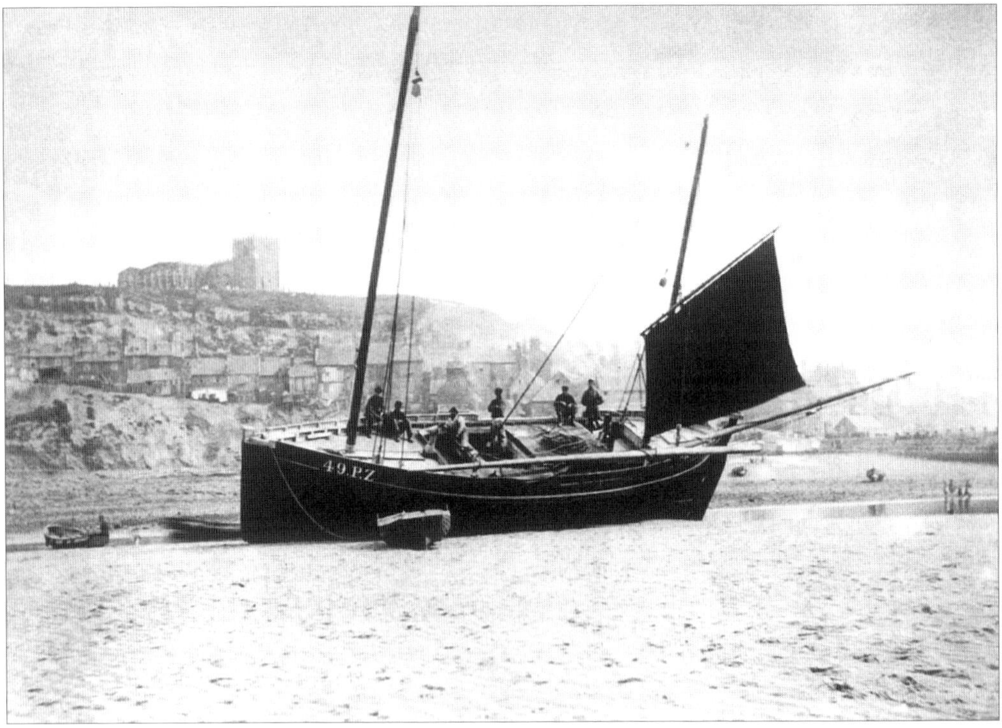

40 'BAGGIE' GOES TO SEA

There was nothing condescending in Joseph's manner towards the fishermen and he was a popular figure amongst them. He became particularly friendly with the crew of the Penzance lugger Joseph *and would often go to sea with them for a night's herring fishing. He dressed like the Cornishmen on such occasions and they in turn called him 'Baggie'.*

Whitby harbour needed frequent dredging to remove the huge quantities of sand that were driven over the bar and, even at half-tide, boats frequently ran aground and so had to wait hours before they could be re-floated. This is what has happened to this Penzanceman (PZ49), although the resulting photograph does give a good idea of its rigging and deck arrangement.

and mules; stately East Anglian drifters; together with fast, sturdy craft from the fishing villages of Cornwall, most of them bearing the registration letters PZ, standing for Penzance.

When the herring fleet was in port a veritable Babel of accents could be heard, coming from the crews of a variety of craft. The Scottish 'Zulus' and 'Fifies' were quite different in their dimensions and rig from the Norfolk and Suffolk boats, and these in turn differed in design from the West Country luggers. It was on such a 'Penzanceman' – coincidentally it was called *Joseph* – that Joseph, 'attired in all respects as a fisherman and known to the crew as 'Baggie', spent many nights at sea, fishing for herring. It was this experience, claimed a close artist-friend, that formed the basis for the painting *In Peril,* that was hung in the Royal Academy's summer exhibition in 1901, 'possibly the most dramatic picture connected with a deep-sea fisherman's life that the artist has left us':

> It is night – a fishing boat anchored. Suddenly out of the gloom looms a great sailing ship – surely she will crush the frail boat! It is a breathless moment! A fisherman rushes forward holding aloft a great torch. One can almost hear his cry of fear and warning! This is virile work, and the studies for it were made absolutely on the spot.[2]

The herring fishery was often referred to as the 'fisherman's harvest', but for most of the year the Yorkshire boats were engaged in line fishing for cod, ling, haddock and skate. While herring were captured in drift nets that hung like curtains suspended from cork floats (indeed, in a sense, the fish caught themselves), line fishing demanded much greater labour. The bulk of the preparation was undertaken by the women, who carried the lines up from the boats, cleaned them, re-coiled them and then baited them with shellfish gathered earlier from the rocky foreshore (the *scaurs*), such as *flithers* (limpets) and mussels, all of which had to be opened and the soft inner parts extracted – and all this in the coldest, stormiest months of the year.

Once at sea, the lines were paid out and marked by buoys (*enders*), then left to fish for a while, before being hauled up and the catch taken off the hooks. It was hazardous, backbreaking toil, and there was many a tragedy when a three-man coble was capsized in a storm and the crew were lost, often within sight of the shore; indeed, in the end it all became too much for Laura and Harold Knight, who decided that they must leave their beloved Staithes. As Laura put it in her

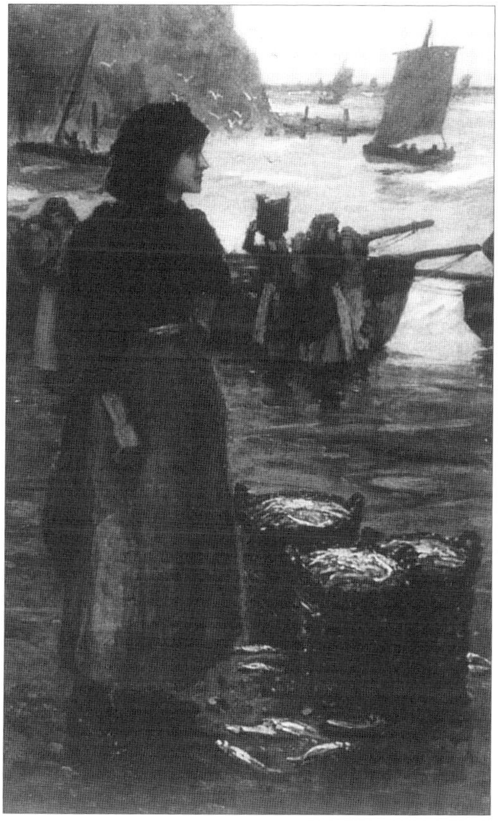

41 'Lives o' Men'

Joseph's main preoccupation was with the fishermen and their boats and gear and their interaction with the sea. He painted shore-based subjects only infrequently and, although he was sensible to the lives and hard work of the women, he chose them only rarely.

The setting for this painting is Staithes; it shows cobles approaching land, while women with baskets of fish on their heads are unloading boats that have beached earlier. However, the main significance of the painting is the young woman, staring fixedly beyond the activity on the shore towards the sea. At her feet are baskets of freshly caught herring, often referred to by fisherfolk as 'lives of men'. There is poignant symbolism here. The woman is wearing a black dress and blouse, and also a black Staithes bonnet – symbols of widowhood. Tragedy too often visited the village, and, in the time that Joseph lived in Staithes, there was one exceptionally heart-rending drowning of a young fisherman shortly before he was due to marry. Quite apart from the subject matter, this is an exceptionally fine painting in terms of its colour and composition, and the young woman's pose is somewhat reminiscent of pre-Raphaelitism.

evocative, acutely observed memoirs, 'We could not contemplate another lonely winter and more tragedies, we were tired of wet and cold: a longing for the warmth and light that we had been assured were in Cornwall came over us.'[3] And so they went, never to return.

There was one other method of fishing that had survived into the early 20th century, principally at Staithes and Filey: *overing*, or 'spring fishing' from yawls, much more substantial craft than the cobles and ploshers. In late spring they put to sea for up to a week at a time to 'fish the off-ground'. They carried nets *and* lines and one or

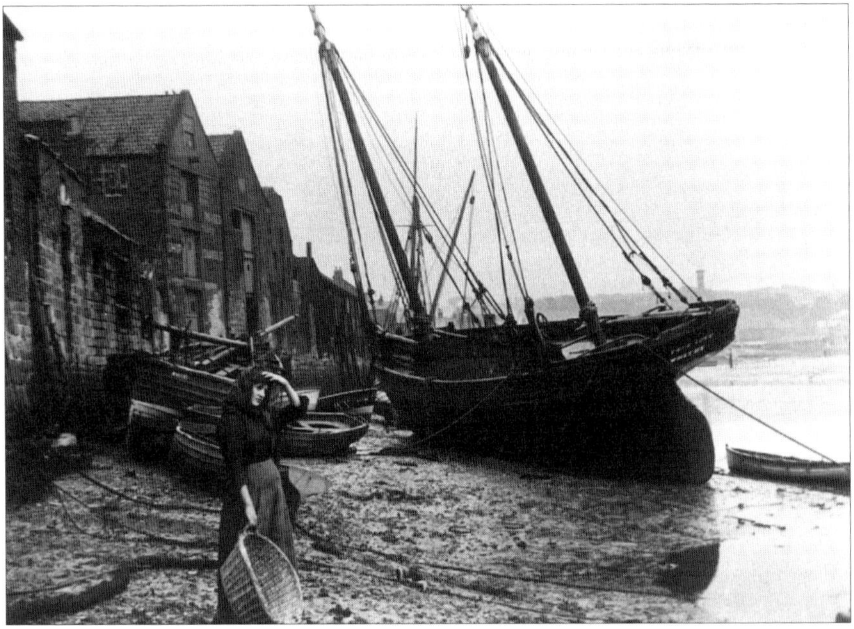

42 FISHING THE OFF GROUND

There were several fishing seasons on the Yorkshire coast. Crabbing was one of them, carried on mainly by the older men. Then, for most of the year, there was long-lining, when the three-man cobles went off to sea for part of the day carrying baited long-lines for catching bottom-living fish, such as cod, ling and halibut. The highlight of the fisherman's year – his 'harvest' – was the herring season that lasted barely two months, August and September, before the shoals moved off south. Between long-lining and the herring fishery, some boats engaged in what was known as 'spring fishing' (or overing). The practice was to shoot a few nets to catch early herring, then to cut these into chunks to use as bait for stout long lines, which were put down from small cobles that were carried on the deck of the yawl and then launched onto the open sea. Early last century, spring fishing was carried on mainly by a fairly small number of bigger boats, yawls, which carried crews of six or seven men and lads.

The yawl True Love *had been built at St Ives in the West Country, but was owned and crewed by Staithes men (the Thompson family) and registered at Whitby. Yawls that fished the off ground were nearly all Staithes-owned, except that the tradition continued at Filey (whose boats were registered at Scarborough). Such was Joseph's interest in the boats and the fishing, and such was the respect that the fishermen had for him, that he was invited by the skipper of the* True Love *to go to sea with them. His experiences were recorded in an illustrated article 'A Week in a Long-Liner', published in* The Yachting and Boating Monthly *of August 1909. Above is a photograph of the* True Love, *taken when, as was the custom, she was laid up for winter in Whitby harbour.*

two small cobles on deck. Often they would sail 40 miles offshore before putting the nets over. If they struck lucky, they might catch several basketsful of herring which would then be cut up into chunks, to be used as bait for the big over hooks. The lines would then be *shot* from the cobles (which were known as *caufs*, that is, 'calves' of the mother yawl) in order to catch the more remunerative cod, ling and haddock. Spring fishing did not last long, but for the women in particular, it was a welcome respite.

It was on board such a Staithes yawl that Joseph was invited to experience fishing the off-ground at first hand, which he describes vividly in an article that was published in *The Yachting and Boating Monthly* under the title 'A Week in a Long-Liner'.[4] The boat in question was the two-masted, St Ives-built *True Love*, crewed by members of the Thompson family (six men and two boys), measuring 54 feet on the keel and weighing 28 tons.

Joseph recalled that when he had once taken rooms in the house of a deceased smack-builder's family when visiting St Ives, he had noticed a faded photograph of a new smack hanging on the wall (*True Love* was registered in 1879). Did the daughters, he asked, know anything about the smack? The vessel, they replied, did not belong to St Ives; it had been built by their father for some men in the

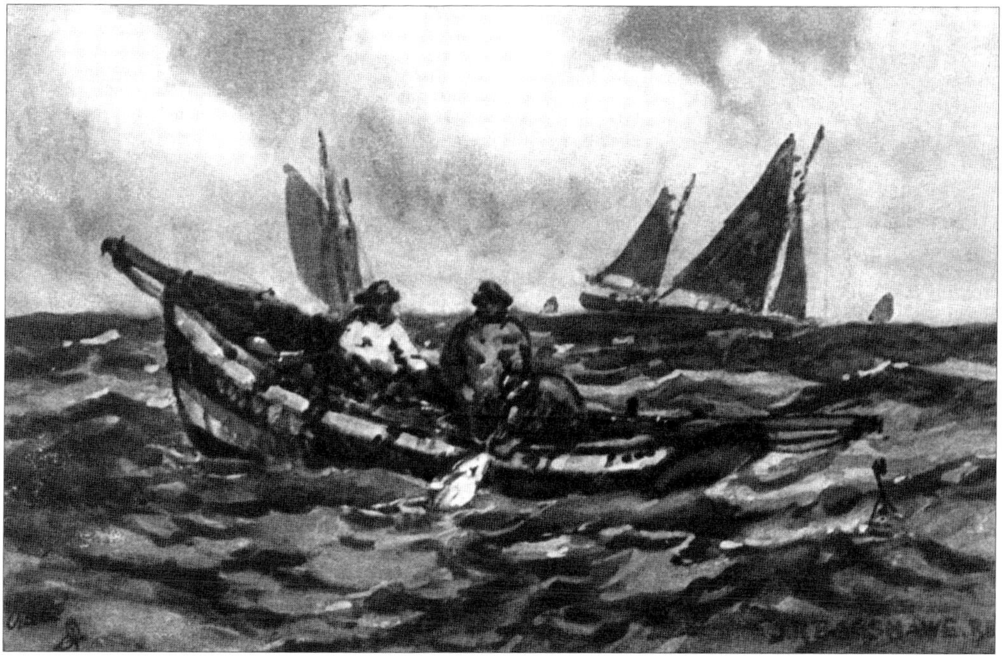

43 Cod-Lining

Most fishing went on either within sight of land or just a few miles off-shore. However, spring fishing from the bigger yawls took place on the off-ground, perhaps even on the Dogger Bank. This painting shows a large cod being hauled aboard a small coble, while in the background is the bigger, parent yawl. It is one of a series commissioned by the postcard publisher Raphael Tuck & Sons. This watercolour is much lighter and more brightly coloured than usual. The treatment of the subject is impressionistic, especially the broad brush strokes that give movement to the sea.

North Country near Whitby, who came to Cornwall to fetch her and stayed in their house. They did not remember the men's surnames, but, they said, they were called John and Matthew. It was probably that same John, known in Staithes as 'Owd John', that now skippered the *True Love* and with whom Joseph had often spent nights at sea in an open coble: it was the first time, however, that he, Joseph, had sailed to the off-ground in the big yawl.

The experience made a deep impression upon him. Without going into pedantic, nautical detail, he provided the readers of his article with a lively account of the spring fishing and of his own subjective reaction to conditions on board. He mentions that he was busy making colour notes for later reference and sketching (the piece is well illustrated with skilful pen-and-ink drawings that demonstrate not only his talent as an artist, but also his command of technical detail). Also reproduced in the article in monochrome is a water-colour entitled 'The Old Skipper in a Squall', which is instantly recognisable as one of the two paintings by Joseph that hang in the Pannett Art Gallery, Whitby.

The trips to the fishing grounds in the *Joseph* and *True Love* were far from being the sum of Joseph's direct experience of the North Sea. There was also the yacht that had been so generously presented to him by Mildred's father, Thomas Turnbull. The brief reference by his son, Wilfrid, to his own father's studying the sea from the fishing craft themselves *and later from his own small yacht* has been endlessly repeated in sale catalogues and elsewhere, but without providing any details. However, in 2004 a water-colour painting of the yacht was discovered in an antiques gallery in Bakewell, Derbyshire. It depicts a trim-looking yacht under sail in Whitby's lower harbour, pointing towards the pier ends and the open sea beyond. In the background are the roofs of fishermen's cottages on Tate Hill and the Haggerlythe, and above them, high on the cliff top, stands the parish church of St Mary. A man and a woman are seated in the stern of the boat. It is perhaps not a great painting, but pleasing and more than competent. Amongst ephemera sold with the painting is a photograph of the yacht, with a manuscript note on the reverse:

THE BEATRICE. JRB's yacht given to him by Thomas Turnbull of Airy Hill, father of Mildred Bagshawe (Mrs B)

The couple seated in the stern, therefore, must be Joseph and Mildred.

The picture itself is signed and dated 'M.W. Freeman, 1901'. Mary Winifrede Freeman had 11 paintings selected to hang at Royal Academy summer exhibitions between 1905 and 1912. During that time, she moved from London to Newlyn, then from there to Bushey in Hertfordshire (where for several years she had a studio), before going on to Great Malvern and, eventually, back to London. There are no obvious links between her and the Bagshawes or the Turnbulls, except that she, too, appears to have been a Catholic, judging by the titles of some of her paintings (for example, *The resuscitation of St Winifrede*, *The dedication of St Edward the Confessor*, *The blessing of the children, Brittany*, *The return of the procession*, and

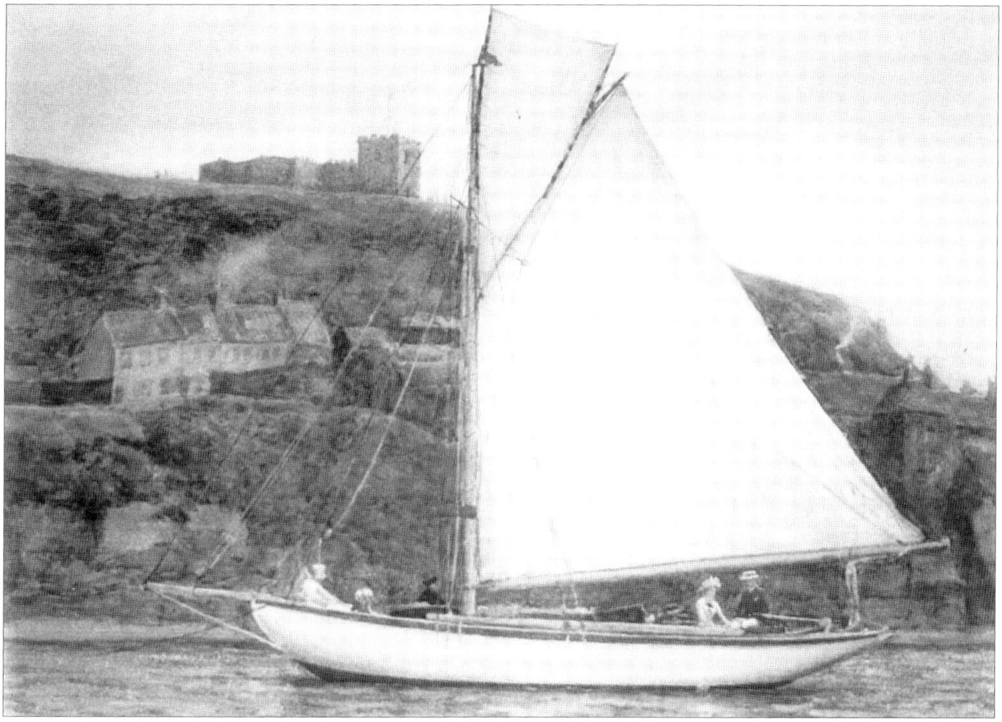

44 THE *BEATRICE*

In a memoir published some years after his father's death, one of Joseph's sons remarked that his father had had his own 'small yacht' in which he went to sea, often for a week at a time and from which he observed the work of the fishermen directly. In 2004, the author came across a painting of that yacht. It was the Beatrice and had been designed and built by one William Day in 1888 at his yard at New Holland on the Lincolnshire side of the Humber estuary. The picture is signed M.W. [Mary Winifrede] Freeman, 1901, and was accompanied by a snapshot of the yacht with the annotation on the reverse: 'THE BEATRICE. JRB's yacht given to him by Thomas Turnbull of Airy Hill. Father of Mildred Turnbull (Mrs B.)'.

The cloister). Be that as it may, the discovery of the painting clears up the minor mystery of Joseph's 'small yacht'.

Also amongst the papers accompanying the painting were a receipt for harbour dues (7s. 9d.) paid at the Custom House, Whitby, for the year 1909-10, together with an official document showing the entry for the *Beatrice* in *Lloyd's Register of Yachts*, the details of which the technically minded reader may find interesting. Launched in 1888, she had been designed by one William Day and built by him at New Holland on the Lincolnshire side of the Humber estuary. Described as a 'cutter', the *Beatrice* was 11 tons Thames Measurement, 30 feet long at the waterline, with a 10-foot beam and 4.7 feet deep; her sails had been made by R. Wallis. In a report of the yacht racing at Whitby regatta early in September 1901, the *Beatrice* is mentioned as being owned by Mr J.H. Harrowing, a member of yet another prominent local ship-owning family, so it looks as if Thomas Turnbull bought it around the time of Joseph and Mildred's wedding.

'Baggie'

During the 13 years that elapsed between Joseph's first visiting Whitby and his death there in 1909, he absorbed an enormous quantity of knowledge about the history of the port and its neighbouring villages, about the people who lived there – their homes and customs, their speech and traditions; about the fishing seasons and the boats and gear employed in the fishery, and about the sailing qualities not just of the local craft, but also of the many varieties that visited the port or fished off-shore in deeper waters. Nor was this all, for Joseph was familiar with the craft of the North Sea generally, and could speak and write authoritatively about the fishing vessels of the Dutch, Belgian and Normandy coasts. Yet despite this wealth of expertise, he was not primarily a social historian or technical recorder of marine architecture: he was, first and last, an artist.

A few critics considered some of Joseph's work to be overly sombre; too dark, they said, too gloomy. However, it should be remembered that a good deal of the fisherman's labour takes place at dusk and dawn, not to mention the hours in between. Also, Joseph was rarely a fair-weather artist: frequently his paintings depicted storm and tempest, landing or launching in roiling surf, or at sea when it was rough and turbulent. This was not just a conceit to inject drama into the painting, but a genuine attempt to portray the reality of the fisherman's day-to-day activity. In any case, far from all of Joseph's work deserves the description sombre,

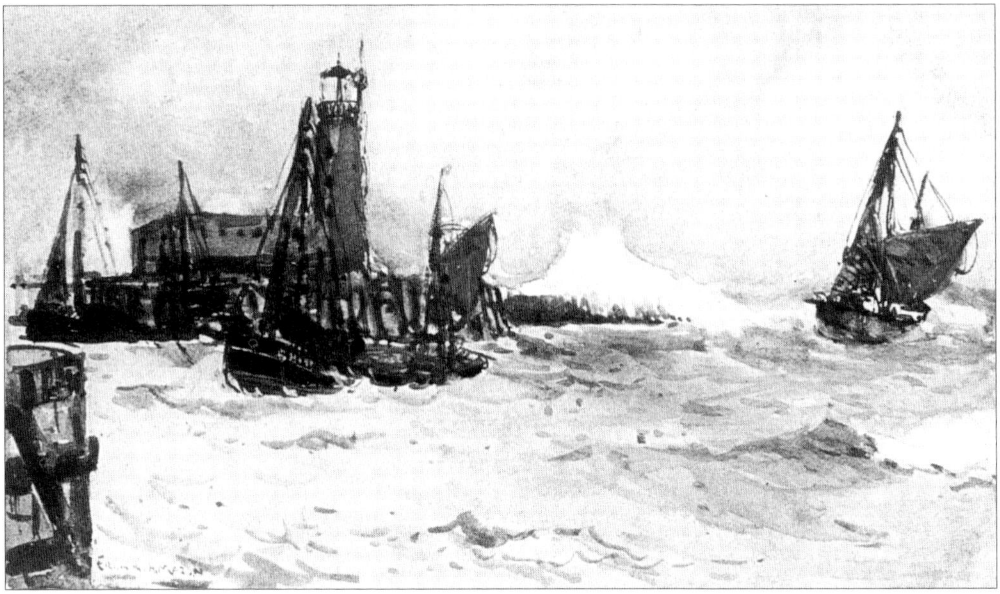

45 *Scarborough – Breakers Over the Pier*, by Frank Henry Mason (1875-1965), postcard

Frank Mason was unusual amongst the Staithes Group artists in that he had actually been to sea. Born at Seaton Carew in County Durham he had been educated on the training ship HMS Conway. *He subsequently went to sea as an engineer, before coming ashore to work in a shipyard. He attended Scarborough School of Art and served in the First World War in the Naval Volunteer Reserve and was appointed an official war artist. Later, he became best known as an illustrator and commercial artist producing numerous posters for various railway and steamship companies.*

since his choice of colour was often subtle and varied and frequently a painting would be enlivened by a highlight that threw the rest of the picture into relief.

While there is no doubting the extraordinarily high standard of the work produced by Joseph's Staithes Group contemporaries – the Knights, F.W. Jackson, John William Howey, Henry Silkstone Hopwood, James William Booth, to mention but a few – many of them preferred to seek inspiration from village life and from the farming hinterland; while of those that painted the fisherfolk, most, as Hirst Walker put it, 'metaphorically "hugged the land" [while] Bagshawe boldly pushed off and made for the open sea. It was six miles from land that his brush most surely found its inspiration; and we may consider the ten years in which he painted the open sea as covering the final unfolding of his style.'[5] This is true, and is in contrast to Laura and Harold Knight's almost comical experiences of seagoing. Argy Verrill, wrote Laura,

> thought we might like to paint hauling up crab pots at sea [...] The boat smelt of fish and everything we touched was wet; it was raining in a mean way. All was grey and cold, the sea was lippy, the coble danced about sickeningly as those endless strings of pots came on board [...] I never saw a scene less inspiring to paint.[6]

Undeterred, Harold bought a leaky old pilot boat, but after several near-capsizes, 'the fishermen, tiring of seeing us take risks, contrived to jam our boat behind their line of cobles at the top of the beach', thus ending the Knights' flirtation with the sea itself.

Joseph Bagshawe was not the only practical seaman among the Staithes Group artists. Ernest Dade (1868-1934), for example, had been born and educated in Scarborough; and had later worked as a deckhand on a variety of craft. Artistically, he was much preoccupied with the movement of the sea – so much so that the sea often dominated his paintings, with a boat relegated to the distant background. In 1933, the year before he died, Dade published a book of drawings entitled *Sail and Oar*. Subtitled *A North Sea Sketchbook*, it contained 100 sketches depicting the seasons of the fishing year on the Yorkshire coast and illustrating the types of boats in use. It is a classic of its kind.[7]

Another seagoing artist was Frank Henry Mason (1876-1975). Born at Seaton Carew in County Durham, he was educated on the training ship HMS *Conway* and later went to sea as an engineer, before coming ashore to work in a shipyard. He subsequently studied painting at Scarborough School of Art under Albert Strange, the head of the School and a noted yacht designer. During the First World War Mason served as a lieutenant in the Royal Naval Volunteer Reserve and was appointed an official war artist (a number of his paintings are held by the Imperial War Museum). Much of his early work is set on the Yorkshire coast, but today he is perhaps best remembered as an illustrator and as a poster artist for several railway and shipping companies.[8]

Dade and Mason both interpreted marine subjects in their own distinctive styles, just as did Bagshawe. For him, there was nearly always a trinity consisting

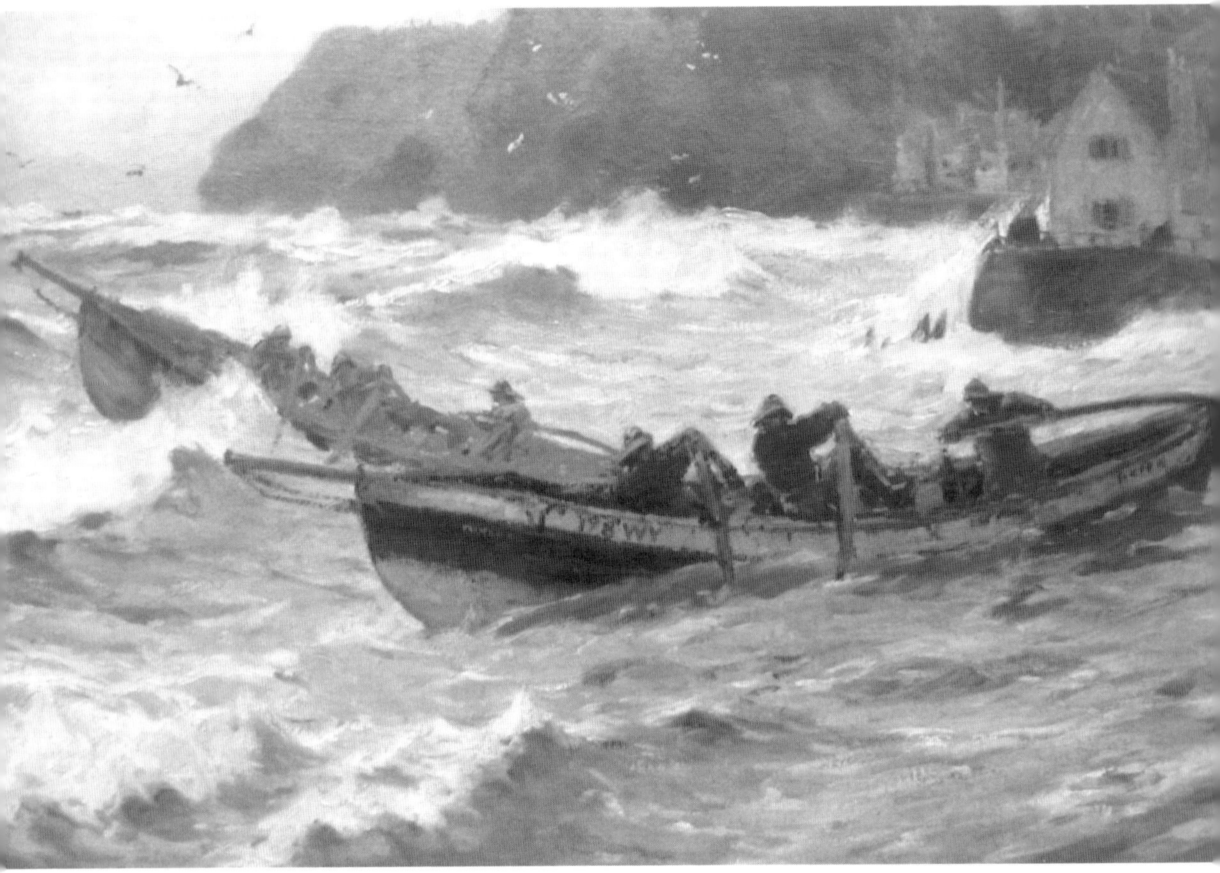

46 Cobles at Staithes

(Above) No-one appreciated Joseph Bagshawe's paintings more than his fellow artists of the Staithes Arts Club. One described him as being 'a mystic of the sea', while another critic spoke of his capturing 'the swing of the seas', and added, 'I think the sense of wave pushing on wave was finely expressed in most of his pictures; he also had the power of making one realise the weight of water'. Wave pushing on wave is the essence of this fine painting, Cobles at Staithes.

of fisherman, boat and the sea 'in its changing moods', with the sea the key to the relationship between these three elements. The sea is never still. Even when it appears to be glassy calm, there is always an underlying movement of ebb or flow. The wind in all *its* changing moods also affects the character of the surface. A rolling swell might be caused by offshore winds, while a storm can turn the surface of the sea into a veritable maelstrom. Bagshawe was a master at creating movement in his pictures. For example, in the dramatic painting *Cobles at Staithes*, two boats are cleaving the waves that are surging towards the shore, yet at the same time we can see the backwash of waves that have already struck the staithe and the cliff beyond and are rebounding back out to sea and thus, colliding with the incoming surf, provoke the even greater turbulence that the three-man crews are striving to overcome. In short, it is the sea that gives point and drama to the painting as a whole.

As regards composition, the boat in the foreground is sliding from the crest of a wave into its trough, before rising again to meet the next breaker and in so doing bares the deep forefoot of the coble, just as in the case of the second boat, which is poised on the breaking crest of the incoming wave at a much steeper angle. The depiction of the rowers is also absolutely right – the helmsmen leaning into the wind while grasping the long tillers with both hands, trying to hold the cobles pointing directly into the incoming breakers (should a boat slew broadside on, capsize would be almost inevitable), while the rowers, each man to a pair of oars, incline in the same direction, giving an overall impression of human strength in combat with the elements. Even an apparently tiny detail such as the positioning of the fishermen's hands on the oars is exactly correct, as can be seen best in the case of the right-hand rower in the foreground: one hand is slightly higher than the other, in order to avoid the oarsman skinning his knuckles (which can easily happen, given the fixed-pin oars). Not only does the artist know from direct personal experience what it is like to be in a coble in such conditions, it is as if he is actually there at that particular instant. All in all, *Cobles at Staithes* is one of Joseph Bagshawe's most characteristic and accomplished paintings.

Perhaps it was this intimate knowledge of tides and winds that prompted one critic to describe Joseph as being 'a mystic artist of the sea',[9] and another to write of him as being one who 'revels in the salt-laden moisture of the open sea' and whose

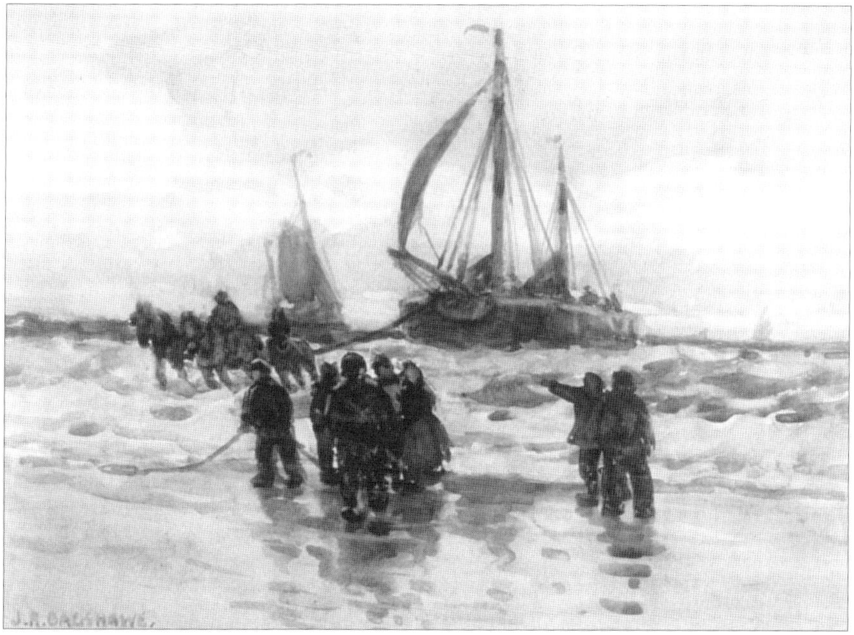

47 *Fishing Boats Nearing the Shore, Holland*

In the summer of 1908, not long before he died, Bagshawe went on a painting holiday to the Channel coast of France and to Holland, where he appears to have been influenced by the work of the Hague School painters, especially Hendrick Willem Mesdag (1831-1915).

paintings are 'instinct with knowledge of the elements'. And Hirst Walker quotes yet another critic who, when reviewing Joseph's work, speaks of the 'swing of the seas' and adds: 'I think this sense of wave pushing on wave was finely expressed in most of his pictures; he also had the power of making one realise the weight of water'.[10]

Following his premature death, and, coincidentally, the winding up and fragmentation of the Staithes Group, many of Joseph's better paintings remained in the Bagshawe family. He retreated into the background somewhat, with attention focusing more on the Knights in Cornwall and various longer-surviving Staithes artists. Only recently has Joseph's work started to become known to and appreciated by a new, wider public. However, during his lifetime some of his paintings *did* come to the attention of a mass audience, for they were part of a curious phenomenon – the worldwide mania for collecting picture postcards.

Six
Toilers of the Sea

The world's first official postcard was issued by the Austrian postal authorities on 1 October 1869. Exactly one year later the British General Post Office followed suit. It was an instant success – so much so that at some post offices the police had to be called to control the crowds. Half a million postcards passed through London's St Martin le Grand sorting office on the first day of issue. By 1879 the annual total of postcards sent via the Royal Mail reached 150 million, compared with 70 million at the beginning of the decade.[1]

Changes in size, format, postage rates and regulations concerning where on the card messages could be written followed thick and fast, while on the Continent illustrated cards came into use quite extensively. A major innovation dates from 1 September 1894 when the British General Post Office decided to permit privately printed postcards to be issued for use with a halfpenny adhesive stamp. However, it was not until 1899 that the *picture* postcard made its appearance in Britain. As the pioneering historians of the picture postcard, Tonie and Valmai Holt, point out, 'The final push that brought the postcard into everyone's home, and sent the annual consumption over the 500 million mark, was provided by the Boer War. Patriotism was a popular sentiment then, and the picture postcard [...] was the right medium to express it.'[2] By 1900, coloured cards were becoming so popular that a 'collecting craze had developed to such an extent that in July of that year the *Picture Postcard Magazine* was published'; and in it Tuck, which was to become the leading British postcard publishers,

> announced a £1,000 prize competition for the largest collection of their cards that had passed through the post, and this accelerated the spread of the collecting habit. Automatic vending machines were installed at major railway stations, special pens were put on sale for the writers of post-cards, portable and permanent cabinets were available to keep cards in, postal clubs were formed with branches all over the world, and many cards that filled the postman's bag were there not to carry a message, but to fill a hole in someone's collection. The Golden Age of the Post-card had arrived.[3]

The subjects depicted on picture postcards were legion. As well as views, there was humour, glamour, actresses, clerics, politicians, cartoons and caricatures,

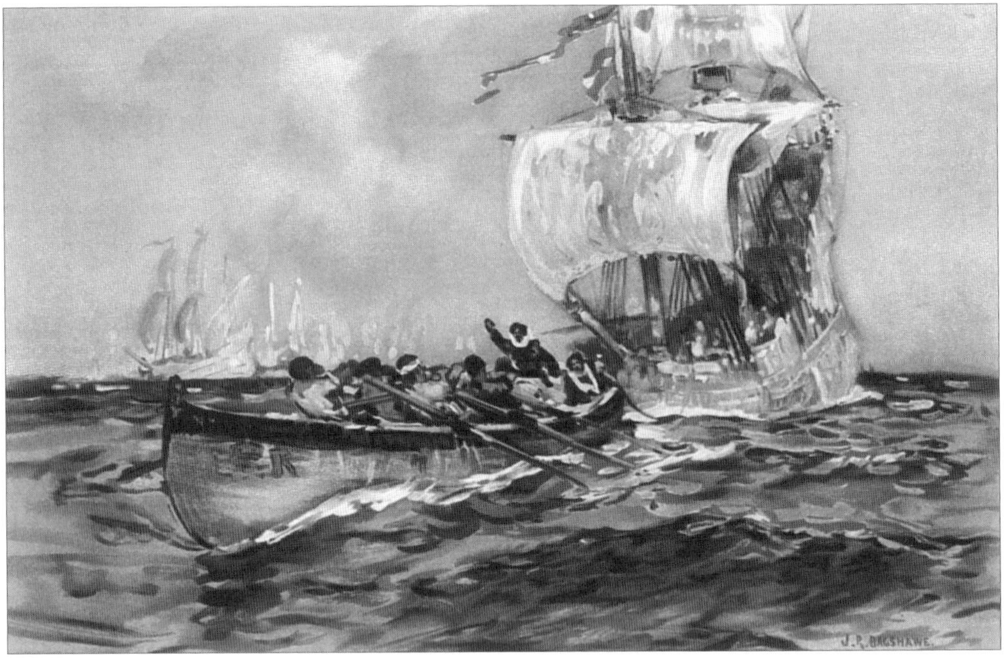

48 *Towing the Prize*
This is one of Joseph's rare 'heroic' paintings and somewhat reminiscent of his grandfather's nostalgia for Nelson and Trafalgar, except that in Joseph's case it was the Elizabethan period that captured his imagination. It depicts a heavily laden Spanish treasure galleon being towed away by an English pinnace. It appeared as a free supplement to The Boy's Own Paper *of 22 February 1908, having been exhibited originally at the Gallery of British Artists.*

advertising, heroes and villains, regiments, battles, tragedies and celebrations, local and national events – indeed, there was little, if anything, that sooner or later did not find its way onto a postcard, and that included facsimiles of great paintings by famous artists. As mentioned, foremost amongst postcard publishers in Britain was Raphael Tuck & Sons, Ltd, whose trademark was an easel and palette alongside the Royal Coat of Arms, and it was not long before they and other publishers began to commission artists to paint local views for reproduction on postcards. Nor was it just the major companies that did this – Tuck's example was soon followed by many of the numerous local photographers-*cum*-postcard publishers who were to be found in every town and in many villages. In Whitby, for example, as well the internationally famous photographer Frank Meadow Sutcliffe (who, incidentally, did not do postcards), there was J.T. Ross, a former shipwright (he had been a riveter in Thomas Turnbull's shipyard) and several others, while at nearby Lythe Tom Watson plied his trade.

Several members of the Staithes Group of Artists spotted the opportunities offered by the postcard mania for supplementing their income, while at the same time bringing their work to the attention of a wider public. One of the first to do this was Frank Mason: a splendid card in the author's collection is entitled

'Scarborough – Breakers over the Pier' and is dated in manuscript 1902 (it also has an undivided back – that is, the non-pictorial side is for the address only – which is one indicator of an early card). Mason also produced sets of paintings of Dutch views at around this date, all of 'watery' scenes, as well as several series of cards of marine subjects, ranging geographically from the Thames to the Tyne.

Ernest Dade brought out a greetings postcard in 1903 bearing a reproduction of a painting dated 1892, showing part of the herring fleet in Scarborough Bay. But a major fillip for northern artists who painted for postcards was provided by J.W. Ruddock of Lincoln who initiated an 'Artist' Series, with every card bearing the legend 'Each picture is a facsimile of an original water-colour drawing'. The Staithes Group painter who seems to have benefited most from Ruddock's innovation was A.G. Stevens, who was commissioned by the Lincoln-based company to paint several series, including Hull, Beverley, Scarborough and Whitby. An item in *The Whitby Gazette* dated 4 April 1904 drew readers' attention to a new set of four postcards by Stevens, one of which was of Whitby's 'famous Tin Ghaut, beloved of artists, both amateur and professional', a point that is neatly reinforced by a gently humourous card that came out at about the same time by the extremely accomplished and renowned Edwardian comic artist Lance Thackeray: it shows half a dozen amateur painters competing for position in the narrow ghaut (alleyway) that led (it was demolished after the second world war to make way for a car park) from Grape Lane down to the harbour side.

Tuck created a hierarchy of postcards, the topmost most expensive category being the gilt-edged Oilette 'Connoisseur' Series, which were 'Processed in Bavaria' – the Germans at that time had the most advanced colour technology, thus ensuring very high-quality reproduction. It was in this category that a series of paintings (No. 2761) by Joseph Bagshawe was published by Tuck in 1907 bearing the title *Toilers of the Sea*. There were six cards in all, all of them depicting marine subjects. It is noticeable that few surviving cards are postally used, suggesting that many of them were purchased by collectors to go directly into their albums. They must have been a commercial success, since they were quickly followed by a second series (No. 2817) entitled *Toilers of the Sea II*, thus making 12 cards in all.

Whether any of the original paintings have survived is not known, but, on the evidence of the postcard reproductions alone, these, almost without exception, are pictures of very high quality. The brushwork is bold and vigorous and the treatment impressionistic. At the same time, the boats and activities depicted are absolutely accurate, even though the artist eschews minute detail. In the painting *A Good Haul* for example (colour plate 7), the three-man crew of the herring coble are in exactly the correct positions and postures, while the coble – that most difficult of craft to draw – is utterly authentic. Moreover, the way the coble bisects the horizon, with the sail of another coble hull down in the trough of the waves, together with the use of colour to define sea and sky, is masterly.

The two series of postcards for Tuck were not Joseph's sole venture into mass culture. In the following year, 1908, an issue of *The Boy's Own Paper*[4] was accompanied as a free gift by a colour print of a painting by Joseph that had previously been exhibited at the RBA. It was entitled *Towing the Prize* and depicts a heavily-laden, captured, Spanish treasure ship being towed by an English pinnace with the royal cipher and ER emblazoned on its bow: in style and content it was more like his grandfather's 'heroic' paintings than of his more recent Staithes-inspired works. This is not surprising, since *The Boy's Own Paper* epitomised the then prevailing nationalistic mood of the country, so much so that 'Boy's Own' has passed into the English language as a synonym for gung-ho adventure, just as, for adults, John Buchan's novels appealed to a wide audience. Not that it was just boys who read *The Boy's Own Paper*: Laura Knight, recalling her childhood, describes the family's gradual descent into poverty and how, one by one, the family's servants left, so that, eventually,

> After the cook went, we had an experienced general [housemaid], and many afterwards who were not experienced, but much less expensive, when Nellie and Cissie [Laura's sisters] had to do a share of the dusting and sweeping, and I became a chambermaid. This I loathed; I was paid only one penny weekly as wages, spent on *The Boy's Own Paper*: I liked reading of adventure and of the things it told you how to make.[5]

On the evidence of Joseph's artistic output alone, it would be easy to assume that his and Mildred's lives were proceeding normally. Every year, one or two of his paintings were hung at the Royal Academy's summer exhibition, and in just six years, between 1904, when he was elected a Member, and his death in 1909, 43 of Joseph's pictures were exhibited at the Royal Society of British Artists. Moreover, he continued to enter paintings for the annual Staithes Group exhibitions and to serve as secretary, before, probably because of increasing ill health, handing over to F.S. Jackson in 1905 (the previous year he had been instrumental in transferring the venue for the exhibition from Staithes to Whitby and the roomier premises of Mr E.E. Anderson's West Cliff Fine Art Gallery in Skinner Street; as *The Whitby Gazette* put it, 'It seems mainly owing to Mr J.R. Bagshawe's enterprise that the exhibition has, this year, enlarged its borders, by adding to the size and importance of the works shown; and we congratulate that energetic and able artist on the measure of success he has attained for the club's effort.'[6] However, since the death of his father in November 1901, when, according to Mildred, the shock had caused him to suffer from 'indigestion' from which he never fully recovered, Joseph's health had been uncertain. Still, life went on, and Joseph and Mildred's first son, Edward, was born at Moss Brow in May 1903, and their second, George, some 15 months later in September 1904. Early the following year, 1905, they moved to a new address in Whitby. Mildred noted in her journal, 'February 16: slept at Old Rectory for the first time'. The Old Rectory (so named because from 1853 to 1873

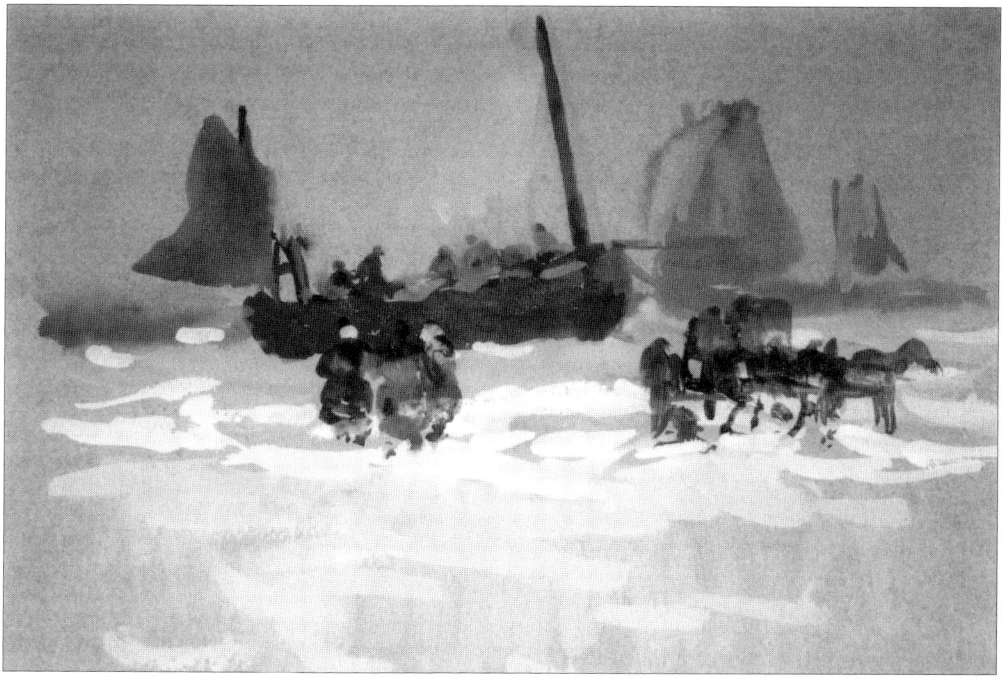

49 WET ON WET

Not long after his trip to the Baltic in a timber ship, Joseph, *whose illness was in remission, set off abroad again, this time to France and Holland with his friend and fellow artist Frederick Stuart Richardson (1855-1934). By now he was employing a technique known as 'wet on wet', where the artist applies watercolour to a surface that has already been painted on and which is still wet. The result is often highly impressionistic, as this sketch of French boats coming in to shore to unload their catches demonstrates.*

it was the residence of the Reverend William Keane, MA, Rector of Whitby, and the vicarage house for the parish), more properly No. 23 Bagdale, is an attractive Georgian terrace house, situated just a few paces away from the church in which they had been married.

In August 1905, Joseph and Mildred let the Old Rectory for the month (a common enough practice in the resort town) and took rented accommodation in Ugthorpe, a moorland village that had once been a centre for Recusant Catholicism, seven miles west of Whitby (where unusually, given his preference for marine subjects, Joseph did a painting of the mill, a distinctive local landmark, and one favoured as a subject by several Staithes Group artists). Afterwards, back in Whitby, Mildred recalled that 'he had his yacht out for the first time this summer [...] I went with him to watch the fleet pass.'

The year 1906 brought both joy and trepidation. Trepidation because of Joseph's being taken very ill at Ardrossan and the Whitby doctor's prognosis on his return that he might expect to live for only another three weeks (so great was Mildred's alarm that Father McCabe, the priest in charge of St Hilda's, was sent for), and

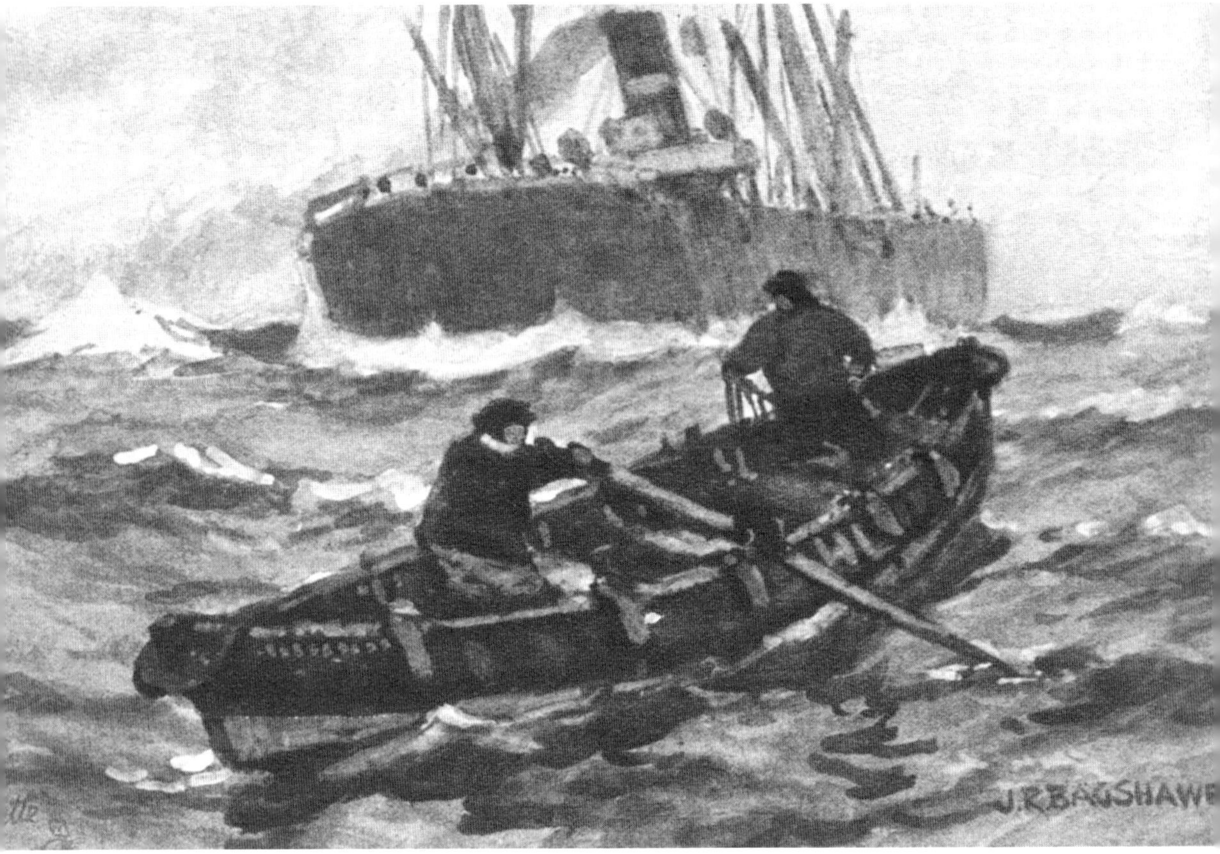

50 *The Pilot Boat*, from the series *Toilers of the Sea*, by J.R. Bagshawe

Bagshawe was renowned for his ability to portray movement. The merchant ship is sailing light (unladen) out of the Tees, so is riding high on the waves. She is wallowing from side to side, while the double-ender pilot coble (Hartlepool-registered) is battling the white-topped waves. The difficulty (and danger) involved in boarding such a vessel in these conditions can be imagined, yet pilot cobles out of Hartlepool on the north side of the Tees would vie with Redcar pilots from the south side, often sailing many miles along the coast in order to secure a ship to take into the Tees.

joy at the birth of their third son, Wilfred. Joseph was way ahead of his time for someone of his age and class. He was present at the birth and, recalled Mildred, he 'helped me better than a doctor' and afterwards 'he nursed me devotedly': 'He used to help so much with the children, bathing them even [and] helping the nurse.'

By adhering to a careful dietary regime, Joseph's health began to improve. At that time, there was no known cure for sugar diabetes, other than trying to control the disease through diet; but by Christmas 1906 he was so much better that he and Mildred 'went to dances, etc., as usual. The sugar went away for three weeks in February, and then, owing to the Dr. telling him he could eat starchy things again, it returned'. A few months later, they heard of a specialist, a Dr Lampe, and went to Frankfurt to consult him in the hope of a cure. 'He did wonders,' and they stayed in Germany for six weeks, returning to Whitby in mid-August 1907 'full of hope'. However, at the end of November Joseph, who was visiting London, became very ill and, wrote Mildred, 'they wired for me'. Folowing this scare, on 16 December they went ot Frankfurt again, and again Joseph's condition steadily improved: they remained there until the beginning of February (1908).

Despite failing health (or perhaps because of it), Joseph entered upon the most intense and productive phase of his artistic life. Later that year, 1908, he went for a 'cruise' (to use Mildred's choice of word) in the Baltic with his brother Edward (who, presumably, was on leave from the army). It would be more accurate to describe it as a voyage, since they were the only passengers on a steamer belonging to Mildred's Ardrossan relations: it was to become the basis for an illustrated article, 'To Russia in a Timber Ship', published in June the following year in *The Yachting and Boating Monthly*.[7] He 'came back well', wrote Mildred. Encouraged, no doubt, by having weathered the trip to the Baltic, Joseph was off abroad again in October, this time with his friend and fellow artist Frederick Stuart Richardson (1855-1934): they went to Katwyk in Holland.

By this time, Joseph was employing a somewhat different technique in his painting, what is known as 'wet on wet', when the artist, painting in watercolour, applies paint to a surface that has already been painted on and which is still wet. This not only makes it possible to finish a painting quickly, it also produces a softer, more diffuse effect than if the first application had been allowed to dry before applying a second. It is a technique that is often used when not a great deal of detail is required. If at the same time bold, broad, brush strokes are employed the result is impressionistic. By impressionistic is meant here not so much the bright, colourful treatments that are so typical of, say, Monet and his French contemporaries (who did indeed use the wet-on-wet technique when painting in watercolour), but, instead, a rather more muted palette, yet one that still *suggests* figures and objects, rather than *describing* them. This departure is most apparent in paintings done by Joseph on the Normandy and Dutch coasts and, as usual, they depict mainly coastal scenes and the local fishing craft. A picture with a saleroom label *Meeting Dutch Fishing Boats* actually shows *French* boats, as can be deduced from the arrangement of the masts (the French and Dutch fishing boats, although very similar in construction, and both having evolved to meet identical conditions, nonetheless differed in the size and arrangement of their masts). However, that detail apart, the picture could just as easily be of a Dutch scene and is reminiscent of the work of Hendrick Willem Mesdag (1831-1915), a leading Hague School artist, who did numerous paintings of fishing boats (*bomschbuiten*) beaching at Scheveningen. Hirst Walker later remarked that, after about 1904, 'we also find the influence of the modern Dutch school becom[ing] apparent in his [Joseph's] watercolour work', and he noted that 'Lady Palmer, at Grinkle Park, is lucky in possessing several examples of this period'.[8]

Mention of Lady Palmer is a reminder that Joseph, like many of his fellow Staithes Group artists, depended to a considerable degree upon patronage in order to sell his work. Sometimes the older established painters, such as Gilbert Foster, Mark Senior and Fred Jackson were able to bring their younger colleagues to the attention of potential purchasers. In that respect, it was fortunate that by the late Victorian and Edwardian periods a substantial number of industrial entrepreneurs were to be found in the manufacturing towns and cities of the North. As Rowland Hill recalled many years later:

> The prosperous cotton manufacturers of Lancashire and the woollen men of the West Riding took a good deal of interest in furnishing their homes in them [*sic*] days. A man who was painting consistently well, and could get in touch with these prosperous business men could always find a ready market for his pictures. There was a great deal of camaraderie among the painters, and while they would quarrel and argue and have differences, their dirty linen was never aired in public. They were extremely kind in doing one another a good turn, and one man often put another in touch with a good stroke of business.[9]

Several patrons in particular stand out. One was Lord Grimthorpe (formerly Edmund Becket Denison) who came from a family that had made its money in railway development. He was a notable horologist, famous for having designed the Great Clock at the Palace of Westminster (usually referred to, incorrectly, as 'Big Ben' – 'Big Ben' is the great bell, not the clock itself): and at the same time notorious for having made a botch of the restoration of St Albans Abbey, so much so that 'to grimthorpe' became for a while a synonym for the unintelligent mutilation of an ancient building under the cloak of restoration.[10] There was also a Mr Lyon of Pontefract; the Hon. Gervase Beckett (a member of the Grimthorpe family), elected Conservative MP for Whitby in 1906, and Sir Charles Mark Palmer.

Sir Charles Mark Palmer (1822-1907) was one of the North East's great industrial entrepreneurs. In the course of his lifetime, from humble beginnings, he worked his way up to become a colliery owner, whence he expanded into the coke trade and from there into the supply of coal by sea for London, to which end he designed and built the first iron screw collier in a shipyard that he had established on the Tyne at Jarrow. He then bought iron mines on the Yorkshire side of the Tees and went on to erect shipbuilding yards, blast furnaces, steel-works, rolling mills and engine works at Jarrow, for which constituency he later became MP, as well as the town's mayor. His company produced warships as well as merchant vessels, and the system of rolling armour plates that he introduced was widely adopted by other builders. Like many self-made men, Sir Charles aspired to having a country estate and in 1902 he came across an almost derelict property, Grinkle Park, on the edge of the moors not far from Staithes (he also had mines in the area). It was Sir Charles's widow (he was married three times) who bought several examples of Joseph's later work.

It was at about this time, too, that Joseph revealed another talent. In 1909, the last year of his life, he began to write, and have accepted for publication, short, illustrated articles in several periodicals, notably *The Field* and *The Yachting and Boating Monthly*. Reading them now, it is obvious that these were far more than pot-boilers to provide a supplementary source of income to support a growing family. They are carefully crafted and written with authority in clear, well-modulated English – indeed it is possible that Joseph would in time have carved for himself a literary career to match his reputation as an artist, had fate not dictated otherwise.

Given the then absence of a cure for sugar diabetes, and the seriousness of the bouts of illness that Joseph experienced from time to time, it is certain that the possibility of imminent death must have been on his and Mildred's minds. Perhaps that is what prompted them to take a short holiday together in the spring of 1908. 'After a few days in town [London]', wrote Mildred later, 'we went to Becca's house [Becca – Rebeccah – was one of Joseph's sisters] in Margate and had another honeymoon.' And, she added, 'he took me all over Thanet' by bicycle, including to Ramsgate, where he had first gone to school, and then, 'last and most delightful to Reculver across the marshes on the high, smooth, grassy dykes [and] we had lunch on the shingle'. There is poignancy in these remembrances, but at the same time a sense of the love and intimacy that Joseph and Mildred enjoyed together.

The geographical focus for most of Joseph's work was the countries bordering the North Sea – the Yorkshire coast, Normandy and Holland. But the Low Countries were not the sole source of overseas inspiration: the west coast of Ireland also exerted a powerful hold over him. It remains a major puzzle as to why Joseph was so captivated by Ireland, although it almost certainly had something to do with religion. Joseph's friend and obituarist, Hirst Walker, seemed to be suggesting this when he wrote soon after Joseph's death:

> A very pathetic interest attaches to a series of Irish studies – works of extraordinary vigour, the last of which was produced within three weeks of the painter's death. These drawings were made during a visit to the West Coast of Ireland. The hand of death was already on the artist, and we seem to feel in these sombre coast scenes the note of sorrow which was soon to fill the hearts of those who loved him. He was among humble Irish friends, who through so many trials had clung to the Catholic religion, of which he was a devoted adherent ...[11]

It is possible, too, that his Irish antecedents on his mother's side may have also influenced him, but there is so much scattered evidence of a love of Ireland and the Irish as to suggest that there were perhaps deeper reasons still to account for it. It will be remembered that his much-praised miniature was of Viscount Southwell, an *Irish* peer, that a Major O'Connor was his best man, and that the honeymoon was spent in Ireland. However, none of the 17 paintings by Joseph accepted by the Royal Academy was on an Irish theme (with the possible exception of *Kelp Gatherers*, which was hung posthumously in 1910 – even so, at that time, kelp gathering was also common on the Yorkshire coast). Similarly, none of the 43 paintings by Joseph exhibited at the Royal Society of British Artists between

1904 and 1909, judging by their titles, was on an Irish theme. However, 16 of the 59 paintings displayed in a 'Memorial Exhibition of Watercolour Drawings by the Late J.R. Bagshawe (1870-1909)' at Walker's Galleries in Bond Street in 1933 were on Irish subjects, mainly of Connemara. Previously, in 1928, Joseph's widow, Mildred, had donated two watercolour sketches to the Tate Gallery; one, entitled simply *Connemara*, is of a traditional Irish workboat, the curragh, but is of only indifferent artistic quality. Some 50 years later, in 1983, Walker Galleries, Harrogate, on the instructions of Joseph's family, auctioned part of Joseph's studio collection: out of 59 pictures only one (No. 40, *Mending Nets in Connemara*) was set in Ireland.[12] Indeed, it has proved to be extremely difficult to trace paintings by Joseph on Irish subjects (the author has one, *Cottage in Connemara*) yet his son Wilfred, writing in 1933, mentions that towards the end of his life Joseph 'visited the seaports of Normandy and Holland, as well as Finland, but second to the Yorkshire coast, it was the unspoiled west coast of Ireland that attracted him most, and his studies of Connemara gained considerable attention and are considered among his finest works'.[13] It is a great pity that apparently none has survived in public collections.

In the same memoir, Wilfred states that in 1909 his father submitted several works to the Royal Society of British Artists, which were 'very well received. But it was to be his last exhibition. He visited Ireland again at the end of the summer, but he was in poor health, and the long journey home to Whitby over-taxed his strength, and he died there on November 1st, at the early age of thirty-nine.' In fact, Wilfred's account is somewhat at variance with that of his mother. After all, Wilfred was just three years old when his father died, whereas Mildred remembered clearly that Joseph had left for Ireland on 20 September 1909 'to stay with Mrs Freer, Ballyconneely, Connemara, Galway', where he had 'felt much better' and had come home to Whitby on 16 October looking 'splendid'.

There was a story still being told in Whitby, almost a hundred years after Joseph's death, that he had dived into the harbour to save a drowning fisherman, as a result of which he had caught pneumonia and died; but that is a myth. Mildred's account, on the other hand, is supported by an item in *The Whitby Gazette* (5 November 1909), reporting his death, which characterises Joseph as being of 'an active disposition, and was very energetic when, last week, he was present at the bazaar of St Hilda's Schools, in aid of the Roman Catholic Church, and took a vivacious interest in the proceedings'. He had also spent a day shooting at Grinkle Park with Mr Palmer, and was driven home in his motor car by Mr J. Pyman. However, towards the end of the week, he was taken ill and 'in spite of all that medical skill could do' he died on the Monday afternoon, the feast of All Saints. Mildred was at his side, and, in a remembrance intended for their sons to read when they were older, she wrote:

> He just turned his head and put his poor tired lips up to me to be kissed and took my hand and kissed it twice and said 'I love you. I love you', the last words he ever said.

Afterword

Had Joseph Bagshawe lived and had he been in good health he would almost certainly have joined the Royal Navy at the outbreak of war in 1914. It is clear from his journalistic writings that he was a keen patriot and even five years before hostilities broke out there are hints that he foresaw Germany as being the likely foe. It is known, too, from his wife's memoir, that his hope was that their three sons would become officers in the Royal Navy, 'the finest profession in the world', although in the event none of them did. For years he had been an advocate of the setting up of a naval reserve and he argued that the fishermen of the north-east coast, as well as elsewhere, were ideally suited to play this role. They knew the seas and how to handle boats and were fearless against the elements; in this his views were similar to those of Erskine Childers, as argued in his immensely popular novel *The Riddle of the Sands*, published in 1903, and in print ever since.

Whether Joseph would have been faced with the same moral dilemma as Childers is harder to say. Childers (1870-1922), born of Anglo-Irish parents, was educated at Halleybury and Trinity College, Cambridge. From 1895 to 1910 he was a clerk in the House of Commons, a period interrupted by service in the British army in the Boer War, about which he wrote extensively. In 1910 he resigned from his House of Commons post in order to work for the Irish cause and was an advocate of Home Rule for Ireland. During the First World War he served in the Royal Naval Air Service and in the Royal Naval Volunteer Reserve; he was awarded the Distinguished Service Cross. After the war, he settled in Ireland and following the establishment of the Irish Free State joined the Republican army, for which he was arrested and shot. John Buchan, of whom there was no greater British patriot, later wrote of him 'no revolution ever produced a nobler or purer spirit'.[1]

There is absolutely no evidence to suggest that Joseph would have thrown in his lot with the Irish republican cause. One of his close friends remembers him as being a staunch traditional Conservative, although not actively engaged in politics; and, in any case, as a *traditional* Conservative at that time he would, presumably, have been opposed to Home Rule. However, his deep sympathy for the plight of his co-religionists in Ireland and the many personal links that connected him to

Ireland and the Irish might well have presented him with a serious moral dilemma had he lived but a few years longer.

In all probability, it was religion rather than nationalism (if one can make that distinction) that fired him most. A public expression of this occurred in April 1908 when the Free Church Council met at Whitby. The proceedings were reported extensively in the local newspaper.[2] In the course of a lengthy speech, the Rev. A.P. Evans of the Bar Church, Scarborough, having first welcomed the Government's Licensing Bill, launched into a virulent, intemperate attack upon the Papacy and the Catholic Church. In response, Joseph wrote to *The Whitby Gazette* indignantly refuting the Rev. Evans's wilder assertions, ending his letter: 'I may say in conclusion that when Mr Evans says of Catholics "there is an insidious influence coming between husband and wife", he is discussing matters of which, by virtue of his calling, he is absolutely ignorant, and I regard his allusion as an impertinence' – strong words coming from the normally mild-mannered Joseph.

Another matter that exercised Joseph greatly was the effect of trawlers on the supply of fish and the livelihoods of the inshore fishing communities. In 1863, even before the application of steam to fishing, a Royal Commission was set up to enquire into the state of the fisheries. One Staithes fisherman, James Fell, told the Commissioners: 'I don't think there is one fourth or one fifth the catch now compared with what was the catch ten or fifteen years ago'. Another Staithes man, Robert Verrill, was asked by the Commissioners, 'What have you seen coming up in the trawl net?', 'I have seen', he replied, 'large quantities of small fish, haddock, codlings, which are young cod, and such like. I have seen the trawl taken aboard on the deck, and have watched them pick the soles, and then throw all the rest over overboard. All that was thrown overboard was quite destroyed.[3] The Commissioners ignored the evidence of the inshore fishermen and gave *carte blanche* to the trawling industry. It would appear that nothing has been learned in the last 150 years.

Although Joseph displayed great sensitivity and sympathy for the traditional fishermen, he appears to have had little concern for the urban industrial working classes, much less for organised labour. Despite his advocacy of the suitability of fishermen for service in the naval reserve, he, like many, many others at the time, seems to have not connected the fact that as many as 60 per cent of volunteers for the British army in the Boer War were rejected for service as being unfit, that there was a widespread view at that time that the population was 'degenerating', and that this might have something to do with the appalling living and working conditions that much of the urban population endured at that time. Be that as it may, his views on such matters probably differed little from those of most of his fellow artists and certainly not from those of many contemporary middle-class professionals. Still, in his personal relationships Joseph seems to have been well liked not only by his immediate friends and colleagues, but also by the wider communities of Staithes and Whitby.

Above all, Joseph was respected and esteemed as an artist. His membership of the Royal Society of British Artists, the frequency with which his paintings were selected for the Royal Academy's summer exhibitions, not to mention his work being hung at a number of provincial exhibitions, are all formal evidence of the quality of his work. But when he died at the tragically early age of 39, Joseph was still developing as an artist; his talent was far from exhausted; and had it not been for his fatal illness, he might have expected many more years of productive work; as his friend and obituarist Hirst Walker put it: 'The death of Joseph Bagshawe in mid-career removed from the Yorkshire coast an artist who had by no means spoken his last word. Many a painter there must be who would have treasured a legacy from his accumulated knowledge of the sea.' *The Whitby Gazette* went further, stating: 'Had Mr Bagshawe been spared [...] he would undoubtedly have won world-wide fame as a marine artist. He possessed the quality of genius – the infinite capacity for taking pains ... As he understood their [the fisherfolk's] lives and their work, so he studied with infinite patience the craft in which they set out to win their livelihood.' Like his grandfather before him, he was a true painter of the sea.

Endnotes

Chapter One, pp.1-16

1. Hirst Walker, 'A Yorkshire Artist and his Work. The Late Joseph Bagshawe', *The Yorkshire Weekly Post*, 30 April 1910, p.15.
2. The account of Clarkson Stanfield's life that follows, unless stated otherwise, is based mainly upon: 'Clarkson Frederick Stanfield, 1793-1867' at: http://www.tate.org.uk; 'William Clarkson Stanfield', *Catholic Encyclopedia*, at: http://www.newadvent.org/cathen/14245a.htm; 'William Clarkson Stanfield' at: http://15.1911encyclopedia.org/ST/STANFIELD_WILLIAM-CLARKSON; 'A Contemporary Notice of Clarkson Stanfield (1793-1867)' at: http://www.victorianweb.org/painting/pva218.html (transcribed from *The Illustrated London News*, 26 November 1859, p.511).
3. I am indebted for this information to Dr Pieter van der Merve, National Maritime Museum, Greenwich, who is a leading authority on the life and art of Clarkson Stanfield and author of the definitive work *Clarkson Stanfield*, exhibition catalogue, Sunderland Museums and Art Galleries (1979).
4. See *The Life of Nelson* by Robert Southey (1813), p.267 in the 2004 Harper Collins paperback edition.
5. Obituary by Charles Dickens in *All the Year Round* (June 1867), of which he was editor.
6. Most of what follows concerning the Bagshawe family is taken from a privately published typescript entitled *A Bagshawe Genealogy. The Descendants of Sir William Chambers Bagshawe and Lady Helen*, by Professor Roy Newton (July 1994), and kindly made available to the author by Nicholas Bagshawe of Rotherfield.
7. See 'Augustus Welby Northmore Pugin', *Catholic Encyclopedia*, http://www.newadvent.org/cathen/12558b.htm.
8. For a detailed account of St Augustine's Abbey Church, see John Newman, *The Buildings of North East and East Kent*, 3rd edn (1969), pp.422-5.
9. Libby Horner and Gill Hunter, *A Flint Seaside Church. St Augustine's Abbey Church, Ramsgate*, The Pugin Society (2000); and Rosemary Hill, *God's Architect: Pugin and the Building of Romantic Britain*, London: Allen Lane (2007).
10. The author is grateful to Fr John Seddon, OSB, archivist, St Augustine's Abbey, Ramsgate, who kindly provided photocopies of the relevant pages from the school's accounts.
11. The description of Beaumont College and of the college regime is taken principally from 'A Catholic Eton', *St James's Budget*, 19 October 1894, pp.20-2.

Chapter Two, pp.17-28

1. Details concerning Joseph Bagshawe's service in the Artists' Rifles are taken from the muster rolls of that regiment held by the National Army Museum, Chelsea.
2. 'Victorian Art Institutions', *The Victorian Web* at: http://www.victorianweb.org/art/institutions.html; and Charles Dickens (Jr), *Dickens's Dictionary of London* (1879), at: http://www.victorianlondon.org/education/dickens-arttrainingschool.htm
3. Hirst Walker, 'A Yorkshire Artist and his Work. The Late Joseph Bagshawe', *The Yorkshire Weekly Post*, 30 April 1910, p.15.
4. *The Wooden Ships of Whitby*, Whitby: Horne & Son Limited (1933), from the preface by Gerard Wilfrid Bagshawe.
5. See entry in E. Benezit, *Dictionnaire critique et documentaire des Peintres, Sculptaires, Dessinateurs et Graveurs*, Paris: Grund (1999).
6. Benezit, *op. cit.*
7. Benezit, *op. cit.*
8. As well as Mildred Bagshawe's journals (kindly made available to the author by the Bagshawe family), she left a 20-page manuscript memoir written soon after Joseph's death and intended to be read by their sons when they were older.
9. Copies of these publications were consulted in the Bagshawe family archive.
10. *Katharine Tynan: Life, Works, Criticism*, at: http://www.pgil-eirdata.org
11. Details of this and other paintings mentioned in the narrative are to be found in: Algernon Graves, *The Royal Academy of Arts. A Complete Dictionary of Contributors and their Work from its Foundation in 1769 to 1904* (original edition, London, 1905), and Angela Jarman (compiler and editor), *Royal Academy Exhibitions 1905-1970*, Hilmarton Manor Press (1987).
12. Hugh P. Kendall, *The Streets of Whitby and Their Associations*, Whitby: Whitby Literary and Philosophical Society (1938), p.40 in the 1971 revised issue.
13. Material concerning James Russell Lowell and other literary figures mentioned in the text is taken mainly from H.P. Kendall, *Whitby in Literature*, Whitby: Horne and Son [no date].
14. Quoted by Alan Whitworth in *Whitby As They Saw It* (second edition), Whitby (2003), pp.41-2.
15. Richard Weatherill, *The Ancient Port of Whitby and its Shipping*, Whitby: Horne and Son (1908), p.443.

Chapter Three, pp.29-42

1. *Horne's Guide to Whitby*, 9th edn, Whitby: Horne & Son (1904), p.129.
2. Nelly Erichsen, 'A North Country Fishing Town', *The English Illustrated Magazine*, no. 31 (April 1886), pp.462-3.
3. Rev. George Young, *A History of Whitby* (2 vols.), Vol. II, Whitby (1817) p.820.
4. John Walker Ord, *The History and Antiquities of Cleveland*, Edinburgh and Stokesley (1846), pp.298-9.
5. For a discussion of the economics of the Yorkshire inshore fisheries, see Peter Frank, *Yorkshire Fisherfolk. A Social History of the Yorkshire Inshore Fishing Community*, Chichester: Phillimore & Co. Ltd. (2002), Chapter 2: Harrowing the Sea.
6. Laura Knight, *Oil Paint and Grease Paint*, London: Ivor Nicholson & Watson (1936), pp.74, 75.
7. 'The American Water Color Society', *New York Sun* (23 January 1881), as quoted by Nikolai Cikovsky, Jr, in *Winslow Homer*, New York: Rizzoli Art Series (1992), p.2.
8. Cikovsky, *Winslow Homer*, p.3.
9. For a detailed description and discussion of the characteristics of the Yorkshire coble, see: Frank, *Yorkshire Fisherfolk*, Chapter 4: Fishing Craft.

Chapter Four, pp.43-52

1. Dennis Child, *The Yorkshire Union of Artists 1888-1922*, Leeds: Leeds Philosophical and Literary Society Ltd. (2001).
2. *The Whitby Gazette*, 19 September 1901.
3. For a comprehensive study of artists' colonies, see: Laura Newton (ed.), *Painting at the edge. British coastal art colonies 1880-1930*, Bristol: Sansom and Company Ltd (2005).
4. All details of Joseph and Mildred's wedding, the guest list and the presents they gave are taken from the extensive account published in *The Whitby Gazette*, 6 September 1901.

Chapter Five, pp.53-64

1. From Gerard Wilfrid Bagshawe's preface to *The Wooden Ships of Whitby*, Whitby: Horne & Son (1933), p.ii.
2. Hirst Walker, 'A Yorkshire Artist and His Work. The Late Joseph Bagshawe', *The Yorkshire Weekly Post*, 30 April 1910, p.15.
3. Laura Knight, *Oil Paint and Grease Paint*, London: Ivor Nicholson & Watson (1936), p.160.
4. 'A week in a long-liner' by Joseph Bagshawe, *The Yachting and Boating Monthly*, August 1909 (reprinted in Gerard Wilfrid Bagshawe, *The Wooden Ships of Whitby*, Whitby: Horne & Son (1933), pp.61-72).
5. Hirst Walker, 'A Yorkshire Artist and His Work', *The Yorkshire Weekly Post*, p.15.
6. Knight, *Oil Paint and Grease Paint*, p.85.
7. Ernest Dade, *Sail and Oar. A North Sea Sketchbook*, London: J.M. Dent & Sons Ltd. (1933).
8. Peter Phillips, *The Staithes Group*, Marlow: Phillips & Sons (1993), p.84.
9. 'Staithes Art Club Exhibition', *The Whitby Gazette*, 21 August 1903.
10. Hirst Walker, *The Yorkshire Weekly Post*, p.15.

Chapter Six, pp.65-74

1. Tonie and Valmai Holt, *Picture Postcards of the Golden Age*, London: MacGibbon & Kee (1971), pp.24-5.
2. Holt, *Picture Postcards of the Golden Age*, p.37.
3. Holt, *Picture Postcards of the Golden Age*, p.37.
4. *The Boy's Own Paper*, vol. 30, no. 1519 (22 February 1908).
5. Laura Knight, *Oil Paint and Grease Paint*, London: Ivor Nicholson & Watson (1936), p.7.
6. *The Whitby Gazette*, 19 August 1904.
7. 'To Russia in a Timber Ship', *Yachting and Boating Monthly*, June 1909, reprinted in Gerard Wilfrid Bagshawe (ed.), *The Wooden Ships of Whitby*, Whitby: Horne & Son (1933), pp.39-51.
8. Hirst Walker, 'A Yorkshire Artist and His Work', *The Yorkshire Weekly Post*, 30 April 1910.
9. 'A Seaside 'Colony' of Painters. Memories of Staithes and Runswick Bay', *The Yorkshire Evening News*, 30 August 1939 (from notes generously supplied by Mr Ian Walker of the Walker Galleries, Harrogate).
10. For conflicting views of Lord Grimthorpe's restoration of St Albans Abbey, see *The Alban Link* (Cathedral and Abbey of St Alban, Issue 63, Autumn 2005).
11. Hirst Walker, 'A Yorkshire Artist and His Work', *The Yorkshire Weekly Post*, 30 April 1910.
12. Exhibition catalogue: *Joseph Richard Bagshawe, R.B.A. 1870-1909*, Walker Galleries, 15-22 October 1983.
13. From the preface by G.W. Bagshawe to *The Wooden Ships of Whitby*, Whitby: Horne & Son (1933), p.ii.

Afterword, pp.75-7

1. Erskine Childers, *The Riddle of the Sands* (1903), notes to the Penguin Popular Classics 1995 edn.
2. *The Whitby Gazette*, 16 April 1908.
3. Quoted in Peter Frank, *Yorkshire Fisherfolk*, Chichester: Phillimore & Co. (2002), p.22.

Bibliography

All the Year Round
Catholic Encyclopedia
St James's Budget
The Alban Link
The Boy's Own Paper
The English Illustrated Magazine
The Yachting and Boating Monthly
Whitby Gazette
Yorkshire Evening News
Yorkshire Weekly Post

Bagshawe, Gerard Wilfrid, *The Wooden Ships of Whitby* (1933)
Benezit, E., *Dictionnaire critique et documentaire des Peintres, Sculptaires, Dessinateurs et Graveurs* (1999)
Child, Dennis, *The Yorkshire Union of Artists 1888-1922* (2001)
Childers, Erskine, *The Riddle of the Sands* (1903)
Cikovsky, Nikolai, *Winslow Homer* (1992)
Dade, Ernest, *Sail and Oar: A North Sea Sketch Book* (1933)
Frank, Peter, *Yorkshire Fisherfolk. A Social History of the Yorkshire Inshore Fishing Community* (2002)
Graves, Algernon, *The Royal Academy of Arts. A Complete Dictionary of Contributors and their Work from its Foundation in 1769 to 1904* (1905)
Hayworth, Peter, *Paintings by Members of the Staithes Group* (2002)
Hayworth, Peter, *From Runswick to Russia. Paintings by Members of the Staithes Group* (2005)
Hill, Rosemary, *God's Architect: Pugin and the Building of Romantic Britain* (2007)
Holt, Tonie and Valmai, *Picture Postcards of the Golden Age* (1971)
Horner, Libby and Gill Hunter, *A Flint Seaside Church* (2000)
Horne's Guide to Whitby, 9th edn (1904)
Jarman, Angela (compiler and editor), *Royal Academy Exhibitions 1905-1970* (1987)
Jordan, Rosamund, *Staithes Group Centenary Exhibition* (2003)
Joseph Richard Bagshawe, R.B.A. 1870-1909 (exhibition catalogue 1983)
Kendall, Hugh P., *Whitby in Literature* (no date)
Kendall, Hugh P., *The Streets of Whitby and Their Associations* (1938)
Knight, Laura, *Oil Paint and Grease Paint* (1936)
Newman, John, *The Buildings of North East and East Kent*, 3rd edn (1969)
Newton, Laura, *Painting at the Edge: British Coastal Art Colonies 1880-1930* (2005)
Newton, Roy, *A Bagshawe Genealogy* (privately published typescript, 1994)
Ord, John Walker, *The History and Antiquities of Cleveland* (1846)
Phillips, Peter, *The Staithes Group* (1993)
Southey, Robert, *The Life of Nelson* (1813)
Weatherill, Richard, *The Ancient Port of Whitby and its Shipping* (1908)
White, Andrew, *A History of Whitby* (2004)
Whitworth, Alan, *Whitby As They Saw It*, 2nd edn (2003)
Young, Rev. George, *A History of Whitby*, 2 vols (1817)

Index

Compiled by Auriol Griffith-Jones

Note: Page numbers in *italics* refer to illustrations and captions; **bold** numbers refer to the colour plates and captions.

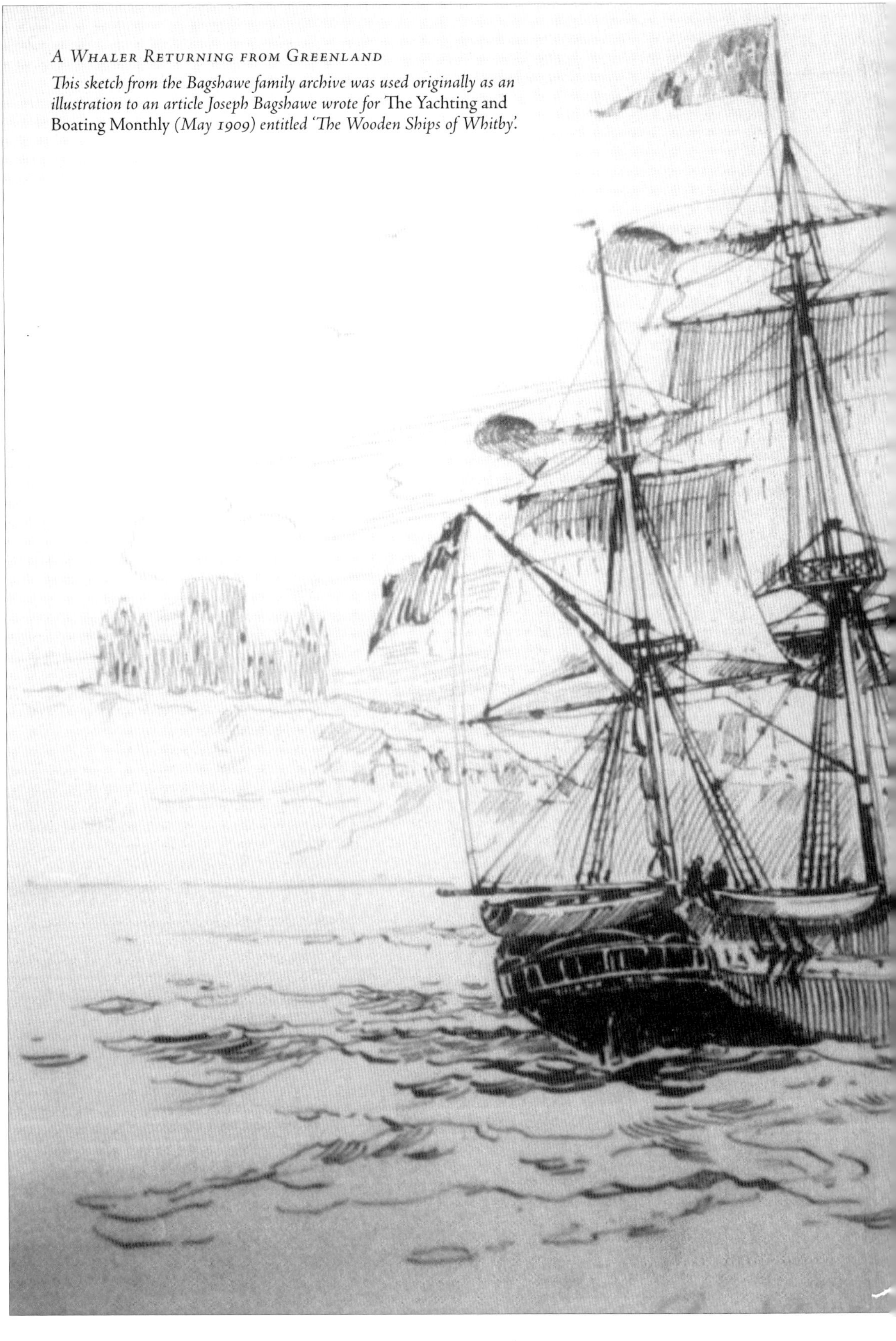

A Whaler Returning from Greenland

This sketch from the Bagshawe family archive was used originally as an illustration to an article Joseph Bagshawe wrote for The Yachting and Boating Monthly *(May 1909) entitled 'The Wooden Ships of Whitby'.*